Consequences for Stepping Up and Speaking Out

CONSEQUENCES
for STEPPING UP
and SPEAKING OUT

WORKING *for the* **DEPARTMENT**
of HOMELAND SECURITY
CUSTOMS *and* BORDER PROTECTION
EQUAL EMPLOYMENT
OPPORTUNITY OFFICE

PENNY DEAN

LIBERTY HILL PUBLISHING

Liberty Hill Publishing
2301 Lucien Way #415
Maitland, FL 32751
407.339.4217
www.libertyhillpublishing.com

Edited by Liberty Hill Publishing.

Printed in the United States of America.

ISBN-13: 978-1-5456-5331-9

This book is written to share my story of being mistreated throughout my life, in particularly by the federal government with the Department of Homeland Security, Customs and Border Protection, Equal Employment Opportunity Office. This mistreatment was based on race, color, sex, height, weight, knowledge, appearance, and because I was upfront and decided to step up and speak out.

The harm I encountered aggravated some of my pre-existing medical conditions. Stress, resulting from my job has caused knots all over my neck, shoulder and back from stress. I have gone to physical therapy, acupuncture, to a chiropractor, and I am still getting massages even though I left years ago. My digestive system had worsened due to the stress. I suffer from a head injury caused by the Executive Director at work; now, I lose information from the long period of stress... wondering what would happen to my career, what the supervisor would do to provoke me, what he or she would say to management to discredit me, and what action management would take.

This book includes the history of the mistreatment. In it I share with readers how it all began, the steps I took to stop their actions, and how I was ignored until I was forced to retire.

Writing this book for me is a means of personal healing, and I hope to promote positive change for others through awareness in the workplace to stop the harassment and hostile work environment and hold managers and supervisors accountable for their actions or inactions.

Dedication

I dedicate this book to my deceased mother and father who brought me into this world to live life right, to respect one another, work hard, and be strong.

I also dedicate this book to my daughters, grandchildren, brothers, sister, and friends who supported me, stood by me, and understood time taken from enjoying the life God had planned for me was due to my concentration on survival and seeking help to put an end to the mistreatment I experienced while working for the Department of Homeland Security (DHS), Customs and Border Protection (CBP), Equal Employment Opportunity Office (EEOO).

Acknowledgment

I would like to thank the very few employees that I worked with for their support and for communicating with me instead of distancing themselves as others did.

One employee at my work location once stated, "Penny, you like your work location, you like the people at your location that you service, you are very close to your home, transportation is not as difficult as in the past, and it is easy for you to get around downtown Baltimore. The only thing you worry about are the people in your organization. You should stay here because the plusses outweigh the minus." It was hard, but it made sense... *if* I could survive until I retired.

Human Resources Manager

Another employee at my work location that knew my situation with managers and supervisors that I work for would come to my office almost every morning to see if I was ok. He used to say, Penny you have always helped every employee who felt they were mistreated and it sadden me for any human to be mistreated in any way when they have not done anything wrong.

Customs and Border Protection Employee

There is an employee from a different work location that stated, "Oh Penny, what you have gone through and persevered. I acquired a great admiration for you when I read your bio previously. This information makes me respect you even more. I am so sorry for the difficulties you have gone through and so in awe of what a successful, charitable woman you have become. Thank you for sharing and know that I admire you. You are a shining example of how someone can rise above the pain and be a light in this world."

Special Emphasis Program Committee Member

I would like to thank an employee for sharing a story that was written about me for Women's History Month related to my experiences in the military as an Equal Opportunity Advisor while stationed in Germany. The article titled This NCO Knows about Discrimination and went on to say:

Penny's whimsical smile and diminutive size might lead you to believe she is a pushover, but she proved she can be as tough as the situation demands.

Penny was the Equal Opportunity Advisor for the Darmstadt Military Community in Germany, and she knows what she's talking about when it comes to discrimination. Over the years, she's faced prejudices about her skin color (even from other blacks who made fun of her light complexion), her gender, and her petite size. But through it all, she has managed to maintain a positive, "go get 'em" attitude.

In her position in the Darmstadt community, she handled complaints concerning discrimination and sexual harassment. Just as the Equal Employment Opportunity Manager deals with similar problems in the civilian work place, she served as a liaison between soldiers or family members, and the chain of command.

"I don't tell commanders how to solve these problems, but I do make recommendations."

You could say Penny has had to pull herself up by her own boot straps. Even after making it through the tough and demanding Drill Sergeant Academy, she still had to prove herself to the commander and other drill sergeants there. They didn't hesitate to voice their opinion that females shouldn't be in that type of job. One even went so far as to admit he didn't like minorities.

However, this didn't dampen Penny's spirits as she competed and won "drill sergeant of the cycle" shortly after completing her training. She wrested the title from a white male counterpart who had already secured the position three times and seemed a favorite for the fourth. "That's when my problem really started," she said. Some people around her made it obvious they were determined to see her fail.

She didn't give up, though. The bigotry only made her want to try harder. "I looked at the male standards and tried to surpass them." And she did. It didn't take long for her to learn to bark orders loud enough to command the respect of all the soldiers in her platoon. Oddly enough, Penny found she faced an uphill battle while assigned as Race Relations NCO at Walter Reed Army Medical Center in Washington, DC. She was faced with a different kind of discrimination this time, though. Because she was just an E-5 at the time, those senior to her felt she couldn't be effective in giving classes to officers.

Her record since coming to the Darmstadt Military Community also tells its own story. Penny was responsible for coordinating all ethnic observances, such as Black History Month, Asian Pacific Heritage Week,

Hispanic Heritage Week, Native American Day, Women's Equality Day, and the list goes on. By all accounts, she had performed very well. Penny wanted to bring Jessie Jackson Deputy Campaign Manager to Darmstadt community. The commander was concern about not having enough attendees at the program because the last few Equal Opportunity Advisors who were males were unable to "pack" the club with their programs. Penny did not only pack the club, she maxed the capacity with 250 attendees and standing room only and had a long line on the outside of people wanting to attend. The commander apologized in front of the audience to say that he did not think Penny could do it.

Bringing Yolanda King to Darmstadt, Germany was another hurtle. The commander told her if she wanted Ms. King as the guest speaker, she would have to raise the money. Penny not only raised enough money to bring Ms. King as the guest speaker, but to stay for a week with her, her family and other military families to share information about her father.

Let's not forget that Penny planned a trip to Spain for Hispanic Heritage Week program taking two busloads of people for a five-day trip. Many people told her that it will not work. They all went to Spain and they all return wanting to know when the next trip will take place.

That doesn't mean it was smooth sailing for her from now on. She knows she'll probably have to come to terms with personal biases in the future, but she has a track record that says she can overcome.

Her advice is, if you think you're being discriminated against, do something about it. "You have to stand up for your rights. It only takes one person to make a change." That person can be you." [1]

Special Emphasis Program Committee Member

I would like to thank a dear person that if it was not for him, this book would not be written. I had many conversations with him. He showed that he cared; he was considerate and understanding. He saw my inner-self and helped me to open up and tear down my "wall," so I could be more vulnerable and less hard and strong, so I could enjoy life with love and fun.

Veterans Administration Medical Professional

I would like to thank a lovely young lady for many years who provided medical services to sustain me through the turmoil of working for the Equal Employment Opportunity Office. She helped me to get to the point of my retirement, because the treatment I was receiving was taking a toll on my heath. She tried to assist by requesting that I be temporarily detailed or place under a different supervisor, but I was denied. She was so happy for me the day I told her I retired.

Veterans Administration Medical Professional

I would like to thank a special person who provided hope and inspiration in speaking God's words to get me through the tough times. I have visited his church, bought his books, and try to watch him every Sunday when I can; especially during the timeframe of my employment with the Equal Employment Opportunity Office. This special person has provided a lot of information to help me to be a better person. I cannot quote everything because it is too much, but I will say this quote: "God wants you to focus on the good things He has for you, which are far greater than the things you can see around you. Unfortunately, too many people give up when they face tough times. They stop expecting anything good to happen. But the truth is, hardships and trials are really opportunities for you to go higher. Whatever struggles you're going through right now, no matter how large or small... they are subject to change." My struggles changed and allowed me to write this book.

Senior Pastor Lakewood Church

I would like to thank my sister who stood by me, listened to my issues, provided advice, and when the ambulance was called that day at work after speaking with the Executive Director when he threatened my career for going to his supervisor, the Commissioner, about his actions against me, she left work immediately and came to the hospital to see me.

Lastly and most importantly, I would like to thank my daughters and my grandchildren for understanding and being there for me. My time that should have gone to them was focused on the supervisors and managers that were trying to take me down by mentally raping me, threatening me, intimidating me, harassing me, and subjecting me to a hostile work environment.

There are many more people I would like to thank, and I am saying it now. Thank you.

Disclosure

I consulted with the Department of Homeland Security, Customs and Border Protection, Chief Counsel Office regarding writing this book and was informed that I could not disclose confidential information in this book. This book is my story about my experiences during my employment with the Department of Homeland Security, Customs and Border Protection, Equal Employment Opportunity Office. There is no confidential information disclosed in this book.

Something about the Author

My nickname is Penny. I was born January 12, 1956, at Freeman Hospital, Washington, DC. At the time, this was the only hospital blacks could go to. My mother told me that my real name came from the nurse who took care of her. However, she "coined" my nickname from the penny she found in the pocket of the robe my father brought for her to wear while in the hospital with me as an infant. Since then, I've been Penny.

I grew up with three brothers and one sister. In my family, we had different shades from dark to light and almost white; I was almost white. Growing up during the 1950s and 1960s, I was able to go many places with my grandmother because of our light skin color, unlike my brothers and sister. I recall my grandmother covering my hair with a hat and taking me downtown, Washington, DC. She put the hat on my head to keep whites from knowing I was black.

Once, when I was young, I went to a neighbor's party. James Brown's record, "I'm Black and I Am Proud," was playing, and I was singing it along with everyone else. A dark-skinned girl turned around, looked at me, and asked why I was singing. She said I was not black. I went home and told my mother. You see, my parents did not raise us to look at the color of one's skin.

One summer, when I was a child, my mother took me, my sister, and brothers to Rocky Mountain, North Carolina to help our aunt and uncle on their farm. What a way to spend the summer. We picked tobacco and corn and fed the chickens, cows, and hogs. Our days began at five in the morning and ended around five in the afternoon. In the evenings, my sister and I would sit in rocking chairs and sing songs hoping our mother would come get us; our brothers, however, were trying to ride the hogs. We took baths in a large tin can, because there was no bath tub as we know it today, and we used the "out-house." There was no indoor toilet. This was a place with just a commode about a half of block from the house. This made us appreciate being home. My parents wanted to teach us to help family and work hard.

As I got older, my sister and I helped our brothers serve newspapers. I babysat my younger brother in the summer and was responsible for keeping the house clean. I attended a Catholic elementary and high school up until the tenth grade when I asked my mother if I could go to a public school to save money, she did not want me to go, but she ended up saying yes. I was able to skip a grade—I began my senior year a year early—because of the curriculum differences between the Catholic and public schools. Looking back now, it's clear this decision was a big mistake. In public school, I learned how to cut class and have fun. I ended up in a fight involving a lot of students. After this, the school transferred me to a different high school for the last half of the year until graduation. I was able to go to the prom, continue working in a work program for the federal government, and I received my diploma, but I could not walk across the stage for graduation.

After graduation in 1972, I continued working for the federal government as a Clerk Typist. While working, I enrolled in a trade school. I could not continue to party, work and go to school at the same time. Something had to go. I needed the job to pay my bills, and I needed the excitement, so I gave up school. I remember partying all night, going to work the next morning, and then going to the bathroom to sit on the commode to get some sleep.

A lot of things happened to me as both a child and an adult. I was molested, brutally raped, and physically, mentally, and emotionally abused. I have the physical scars even today. I did a lot of things I am not proud of while growing up. A family friend once commented that I should move away because if I didn't, I would either die or go to jail.

I decided to join the military, even against my father's wishes. He served during WWII and witnessed the treatment of women then. My recruiter reassured him that times had changed. When Dad heard I would have an opportunity to go to school, he was sold. I told my sister and we both entered the Army, and left for basic training at the Women's Army Corps, Fort McClellan, Alabama in 1975. I remembered my mother saying to my sister and I that she raised strong black girls, and we were going to be alright. After basic training, I went to Germany and my sister went to Chicago.

During my military career, I served as an Administrative Specialist, Personnel Specialist, Drill Sergeant, Race Relations Instructor, Equal Opportunity Advisor, and was trained by Equal Employment Opportunity Officers to perform their duties and responsibilities.

I recall, as an Equal Opportunity Advisor eleven to thirteen soldiers spoke with me about issues with the Deputy Commander. I took their complaints to the Commander; he had a meeting with my supervisor, Deputy Commander, and myself and found that the allegations were true and took action. For my speaking out on behalf of the soldiers, I received a lower rating on my performance rating from my second-level supervisor, the Deputy Commander. Instead of receiving 125, which is the highest rating for doing my job and beyond, I received 118 because I brought the soldiers complaints to the attention of the Commander. I filed no complaint against the Deputy Commander for giving me a low rating, even though my performance did not deserve that lowered rating. I sucked it up and kept on moving to bring no attention to me. You see, the military was my family, and I wanted to be all I could be. Therefore, I did not step up and speak out. Plus, I was taught what goes on in our house, stays in our house. Meaning, within self.

Later, I found out about a school that "stamps out discrimination," the Defense Race Relations Institute. I thought about what happened to me when I was growing up, about getting in fights because of my skin color, being called reds, red bone, and high yellow; I also reflected on the turmoil in the United States regarding race relations, having to prove myself because of my sex, and what the Deputy Commander did to my rating and decided to apply to the Defense Race Relations Institute. I was accepted, attended, and I graduated. I hoped the training combined with my experiences would help me make a difference and help others who were mistreated.

In 1997, I retired from the United States Army after twenty-two years of service as a Master Sergeant. I was not ready to retire. I remember being stationed in Germany and my Command Sergeant Major called me to say that he had a great assignment for me at the Pentagon working for the Equal Employment Opportunity Office. When I retired, I could walk right into a civilian job. It sounded great. I would have a civilian job, my daughters would get to know our family, and I would be back home. My daughters liked Germany and did not want to leave, but I thought this would be a great opportunity. I was wrong.

I was the only military personnel in this office of civilians and a Black-American female supervisor. This supervisor did not want me to do my military job. She wanted me to cater to her civilian employees, make copies, help with their programs, take equipment to different offices, and so on. Because I spoke out about my job, I was moved from her office to an area that had a desk and chair with water dripping down from the ceiling and no one else around. I was a Master Sergeant that could not take care of the military personnel and do my military job. This was a disgrace. I woke up on April Fools' Day and decided to submit my retirement papers. People thought I was joking because of the day I chose, but I was serious. I had a civilian supervisor for the first time that knew nothing about the military. What she cared about was having the first-time military personnel to supervise to receive a promotion.

After I retired, I attempted to open a youth community center in my community. During this time, there was no place for the young to go except the corner. I had the support of the police department and the congressperson, but not the support of the community. Therefore, I could not move forward.

I became a substitute teacher at the middle school where my children attended. I remembered being a substitute teacher for one of my daughter's classes. She raised her hand and said "Mom." I responded, while we are in class, you will address me as Ms. Penny.

I was also a foster parent. I opened my house to the kids in the neighborhood, took them on trips, and had sleep overs.

I contacted different organizations to volunteer to put together an event for veterans in helping them in a different way: no retreats, no group meetings, no individual meetings that all help with mental and physical issues, being alone, loosing family members because of time in the military, and others. I wanted to do something different. I asked If I could put together a "Veterans Finding Love" event. I believe love can take a veteran to the next level of recovering and feeling good about themselves. Love brings continuous happiness, excitement, fun, communication, understanding and that will help the veteran to move beyond. I thought this was a good idea. I was told this was a good idea, but no one came forward to say, let's do it.

I bought each of my daughters a home to teach them homeownership, and I bought my brother one too, so he could help me with our oldest brother. Later, the economy changed. My family members moved out of the houses, and I rented the properties. I became an owner, landlord and property manager. What came with this responsibility was losing a lot of money through tenants not paying rent, court fees, laws, rules and courts favoring tenants, evictions, properties not rented, and tenants damaging the properties. What a life.

I decided to reenter the federal government as an Equal Employment Opportunity Specialist. My sister had mentioned to me that the civilian world was not like the military. She said, "It is a dog eat dog world" in the federal government.

My first job was an Equal Employment Opportunity Specialist in Patuxent River, Maryland. It was about two-and-a-half hours from my home. Due to the driving time required to get to and from work, and because the supervisor at the time was leaving, I decided to look for another job. I really liked that supervisor. She allowed me to have freewill to do my job. I did a great job, and she awarded me. However, it was another employee, a Hispanic female who thought she should have received an award when she did not. I did not realize she had an issue until she applied for the supervisor's position and got it. Because I got the award while she felt she deserved it, she made my job very hard to perform. Therefore, I found another job as an Equal Employment Opportunity Specialist in Aberdeen, Maryland.

This job was an hour away, the commute was much better, and this was a small office. Everyone, including the supervisor, seemed to get along, and I enjoyed my job. All was well until the supervisor left for medical reasons or retirement; I cannot recall. What I do remember is that a disabled white female in a wheelchair became the acting supervisor. Soon, all hell broke out with the acting supervisor and the other employees. This supervisor got a white male fired, and she made it hard for all of us in the office until we decided to leave. I do not know what happened when I left. I just know a few employees left around the same time I did. It made me wondering what was going on with the Equal Employment Opportunity Office. If *any* office should be doing their job by taking care of its employees, it should be the Equal Employment Opportunity Office. That's what it stands for. One would expect it to be the best place to work.

I found a job with a promotion as an Equal Employment Opportunity Specialist in Washington DC, working in the formal stage of complaints. I found myself in the same situation with my commute; however, this time I drove to the train station, caught the train, got off the train, caught the metro, and then I walked to work. Imagine the time to-and-from work in traffic Monday through Friday.

I remember my first day walking into the office. A Black-American female secretary asked me my race. I was surprised. I asked her what did she think it was. She responded with every race except black.

I came to work every day wearing a suit and heels. There were between eleven and thirteen Black-American females who worked in the same office with me; I was the lightest one, and there was one white male. I recall the white male saying he was glad that I was there. I asked no questions, and kept it moving.

In learning the job, management informed me to work with the employees. I would turn in my work to the supervisor, and it was wrong. I wondered why the employees who had done the work for long periods of time and knew the work would give me incorrect information. I learned fast not to depend on anyone else to help me learn how to do the job.

Everybody was over worked and had a large load of Equal Employment Opportunity cases. As a new employee, I had between fifty-two and sixty-seven complaints. Others had many more. My original supervisor left, and we got a new one. This supervisor was a Black-American male and a military retiree. I liked how he did business. He came in and spoke with the employees separately, researched other agencies' best practices, spoke with us in a group, and asked for feedback. Afterward, he gave his decision on how the office was going to be ran and his goals. I went from fifty-two to sixty-seven cases down to eleven to thirteen within a year. After years of working in Washington DC, I was growing tired of the commute, so I decided to look for a job closer to home.

One day, I saw a position on USAJOBS for an Equal Employment Opportunity Counselor with Department of Homeland Security, Customs and Border Protection, Equal Employment Opportunity Office, Baltimore, Maryland. I applied for the position and was hired. I was happy because this job was close to home, and it was one job, a counselor, after many years of having many responsibilities.

Contents

RECOMMENDATIONS

Getting to Know My Work Environment

My office was located in Baltimore, Maryland with employees of the Baltimore Field Office. My chain of command and coworkers were not physically located with me. This was an ideal location; it was close to home and located in an environment that I could go out and walk during lunch time. I was working in a location with good people, and was able to perform my "one" job with less interruptions.

This "one" job did not last. I ended up managing the Informal Complaints, Investigating Complaints, Special Emphasis Program, Disability Accommodation Program, Religious Accommodation Program, Outreach Program, Community Outreach Program, Alternative Dispute Resolution Program, Site Visits, Training, and all other duties assigned of areas of responsibility that changed to often.

I had about thirty-six years of doing the job as a Race Relations Instructor, Equal Opportunity Advisor, and Equal Employment Opportunity (EEO) Specialist. I think I knew how to do my job. As a matter of fact, I believe I had more experience coming into this EEO Office than any other employee to include supervisors and managers.

I learned that this job was not a thinking job. It was a robot job. I was told what to say and do for all aspects of the job. Based on my experience working for the EEO Office, the Executive Director, a short Black-American male did not know how to run the office. The office name changed, positions changed, title changed, supervisor changed, duties changed, structure changed, and duties and location of responsibilities changed on numerous occasions in a short period of time. Employees were leaving the job and taking lower grade jobs to leave because of the Executive Director's poor management of the office and his mistreatment of some of the employees.

Now, if you recall, I said "a short Black-American male." I said this because the Executive Director acted as if he had a complex because of his height by how he acted, walked, and talked; he thought he was the "man." He thought he was God's gift to the world. He knew it all, had done it all, and no one could touch him. If you know short men—some of them, not all—who are in a position of power, check them out. My experience is that you cannot tell them anything, especially if you are a lady who knows your stuff.

The treatment that I suffered in this office is not an isolated one. It happens across the federal government. Employees have retired for a new life, skipped around to other federal agencies in hopes of a new start; some have filed class action suits, which take many years to go through the process, because the agency will prolong them. Even worse, some have committed suicide, because they could not deal with the treatment. Still others are silent in order to bring no attention to themselves.

The EEO Office that I worked for was separated into three sections: Informal Complaints, Formal Complaints and Privacy Office. The employees working under the Informal Complaints, which I was, had more responsibilities in comparison to the other sections. Every time another area was short, the employees were pulled from Informal Complaints.

We used to complain about the Executive Director hiring more people for the Privacy Office and Formal Complaints. Yet, in Informal Complaints, he would not hire employees who could step in and do the job. He hired employees at lower grades who had college degrees with no or very little experience in EEO to save the agency money. I know this, because we had to train them. I call this power and control for advancement. We, as employees, complained to one another about the Executive Director taking on responsibilities knowing we did not have the manpower, just to make himself look good, to help his resume, and to receive monetary awards. With my history with the Executive Director, I believe it was about him, not his employees who did the job, at least not unless he liked you.

I worked for this Executive Director for nine years, and with each complaint that I filed, whether verbal or in writing, his actions toward me and his supervisors and managers were against all policies to ensure my work environment was one of equality, fairness, and respectful treatment.

Customs and Border Protection Commissioner's Message

All Customs and Border Protection employees have the right to work in an environment free from discrimination and harassment. Every Customs and Border Protection (CBP) employee is responsible for ensuring this happens. Join me in fostering an environment of equality, fairness, and respectful treatment of our co-workers, job applicants and the public we serve. Pledging to uphold these values helps us succeed in maintaining integrity, vigilance and service to our country.

Customs and Border Protection Deputy Commissioner's Message

All CBP executives, managers, and supervisors should take immediate and appropriate action once they are made aware of an allegation of harassment. Please note that even if an individual's behavior does not rise to the level of unlawful discrimination as defined by federal law, regulation, executive order, or policy, it may still violate CBP's Standards of Conduct.

The military taught me to resolve issues at the lowest level. In all of my complaints, I started with my immediate supervisor and then my second-level supervisor, the Executive Director, and received no help to stop the harassment behavior that made my work environment hostile.

Since I filed complaints, the Executive Director decided to add a second-level supervisor to make him a third-level supervisor to look like he had nothing to do with his managers' behavior toward me. I filed more complaints, and he got himself a Deputy Director. Again, to look like he was not involved in actions against me. The Executive Director knew exactly what was going on in his office, and his managers could not do anything without his approval. I was not the only one who was filing complaints against the Executive Director, but I was one who only a hand full of employees would talk with. The others would not talk unless they wanted information to go back to management to make them look good.

I knew my job, and I did it well. I got a lot of cases, because I resolved the majority of them instead of having them go through the Informal Complaint process. I give enough information to employees for them to make the decision to file or not. That was the key "to educate."

I have requested help to cease and desist management's behavior toward me through my chain of command to include the CBP Commissioner, Department of Homeland Security (DHS) Secretary, Internal Affairs, Inspector General, Joint Intake Center, Office of Special Counsel, Worker's Compensation, Congressperson, former Attorney General, and the former President of the United States and the Commander in Chief with no help: the behavior continued.

I sent a letter to the former President of the United States. The subject was titled "HELP: Demand Peace from Your Leader," and stated the following:

Just recently, you completed an overseas trip and one of the places you visited was Israel. During your stay, you informed the students to "demand peace from your leader." I am using your quote to demand your help for peace in my workplace. I provided my personal information and my work location. I stated the actions taken against me and others because I exercised my right to file complaints against management.

The former President referred my complaint to the EEO Commission (EEOC) for them to respond to me. They stated that I had a hearing pending.

I needed management's behavior to stop then, not later, and especially not after more actions were taken against me. I continued looking over my shoulder for the next harmful action until I was forced to retire. By upper management not ensuring the behavior ceased, they gave the Executive Director permission to continue treating me unfairly. If upper management would get involved, like my earlier experience in the military of the Commander calling the parties in for a meeting to discuss the matter to resolve it, it would save a lot of time, money and the employees would work in a healthy work environment. Instead, they hear one side — the side of the manager who is causing the problem.

I know every office, organization, or agency is not perfect, I get that, but working in an organization that knowingly allowed me to stay in a hostile work environment to the point of the Executive Director intimidating and threatening my career and passing out, should not be allowed. I only wanted to do my job. Because I stood up and spoke out about a manager disrespecting my supervisor in front about sixty-seven employees started the emotional roller coaster that would not stop until I was forced to retired.

I was emotionally raped, intimidated, bullied, and threatened. Therefore, since I could not get help to stop the treatment I encountered working for this office, I decided to write this book with my experiences and facts in hope that a change would take place that employees voices can be heard when mistreated, and action taken to correct the behavior.

Based on life experiences, I became strong on the outside, yet caring; I'm a hard worker and upfront. I am real, and I keep it real. I think that is what the managers and supervisors did not like, me stepping up and speaking out.

Let me tell you about my concerns, the issues or complaints, whether verbal or written (some I discussed with management) that will show what happened to me in this office. You may overlook one, two, or maybe three issues, but when the actions continued while every investigation conducted found nothing against me, you have to wonder if this was personal when I was doing my job and did not receive a Performance Improvement Plan so that I would eventually be terminated. I am not including the dates of the incidents or names, just the actions taken against me, because that is the most important take away.

Complaint 1

Intimidated for Stating "Filing a Harassment Complaint" Against a Supervisor

I attended an annual Equal Employment Opportunity (EEO) conference in Washington, DC, with about sixty-seven employees, supervisors and the Executive Director from our office, the EEO Office regarding our duties and responsibilities. This was an opportunity to meet coworkers, supervisors, and managers and to find out more about my new job since this was my first week on the job.

During this conference, Supervisor 1 spoke to us, and part of her conversation included negative comments about Supervisor 2, my supervisor. I thought the comments were unprofessional, inappropriate, and it was just wrong to speak negatively about a supervisor in that forum. I cannot remember the exact words today, but it concerned me that one supervisor would talk down about another supervisor in the same organization with her employees there when this supposed to be a learning conference. I was sitting upfront, and I turned around to look at Supervisor 2 to see if she looked alright. I thought, *if this is happening to a supervisor in this forum, what have I gotten myself into?*

After the conference, I received an evaluation to complete regarding the conference via email. I am an upfront and "real" person, and I knew if the survey asked me questions regarding how I felt about the conference or something similar, I was going to be honest. Therefore, I spoke with Supervisor 2 and told her I was unable to complete the evaluation unless I told the truth about how Supervisor 1 disrespected her by making unprofessional comments—if that question came up. She told me not to complete the evaluation. I asked what would happen if I received another one. Supervisor 2 stated that the evaluations were confidential, so they would not know if I sent one in or not.

Later, I received another evaluation to complete. I contacted Supervisor 2 again and stated that I was unable to complete the evaluation unless I told the truth about the comments Supervisor 1 made about her in the group. Supervisor 2 told me to complete the evaluation or I would receive another one. I could not understand how I could receive another survey, if the survey was confidential. How did they know if I had submitted one or not? The Executive Director knew, though, because the surveys were returned via email. I completed the evaluation and made the statement that Supervisor 1's comments to Supervisor 2 (in front of about sixty-seven employees) were unprofessional. I had a choice: either say something or not, and I thought the right thing to do (if I *had* to complete the evaluation) was be honest.

The Executive Director had a meeting with his supervisors to discuss the evaluations. Little did I know the relationship the Executive Director had with Supervisor 1 in the workplace. They reviewed the evaluations, including my own. Both my name and what I stated was addressed. I know this because Supervisor 2 informed me of it, and the evaluation was sent back to me to complete via email. They had my name.

From that point on, Supervisor 1 began to harass me through telephone conversations when she filled in for Supervisor 2. I informed Supervisor 2, and she told me that she must report the harassment to the Executive Director, which she did. The Executive Director contacted me. Instead of speaking about the harassment, he stated that he knew Supervisor 1, and that she would not harass me; he also told me that I did not complete the Outside Employment Application, which I did. I informed the Executive Director that I would not file a complaint. I got the message loud and clear. Supervisor 1 was upset with my statement about her, and the Executive Director did not like the fact that I was going to file a complaint against his friend and manager. I informed Supervisor 2 that all I wanted to do was my job, and I did not want any problems. I thought this matter was resolved because I did not file a complaint. This is when my problems started; managers were not able to let it go, and move on.

2. Supervisor 1 said as the Counselor of record, I should not have sat in an observed. I asked how I could have known this because there was no written documentation or information provided in training or conference calls that a counselor should not observe mediation.

3. Supervisor 1 said my attending mediation was inappropriate attendance and participation. How could this be inappropriate attendance when I was not notified that I could not attend mediation until after the fact? And I did not participate in this mediation as Supervisor 1 said, I only "observed."

4. Supervisor 1 said I asked Director, Baltimore Field Operations to attend the mediation. My response indicated that I did not ask Director, Baltimore Field Operations if I could attend the mediation. I asked if he needed anything for the mediation. He asked me to attend and introduce him and counsel. Supervisor 1 had a tendency of changing my words to benefit her.

5. Supervisor 1 said I failed to seek her approval to attend mediation. I did not know if I needed Supervisor 1's approval, when the person that I serviced requested my attendance, and there was not enough time to request Supervisor 1's approval prior to mediation. I did let her know what happened after the mediation.

6. Supervisor 1 said attending mediation was a conflict of interest. I responded that conflict of interest is any relationship that is or appears to be not in the best interest of the parties. A conflict of interest is when a Complainant files a complaint against me; an investigation is conducted; I submit a statement based on the complaint; questions on how I processed his complaint are asked; answers are given; documentation is submitted, and I have to counsel his complaint prior to the results of the investigation. I asked Supervisor 1 if it was a conflict of interest for me to process the Complainant's complaint when he filed a complaint against me, and I received no response.

7. Supervisor 1 said that maintaining confidentiality was an important component of the Alternative Dispute Resolution process, which I maintained.

8. Supervisor 1 said those "serve neutrals" for the Commissioner should be precluded from performing, investigating, or enforcement functions. My response was that I was not an investigator, and I could not enforce any functions.

9. Supervisor 1 said I commented that the employee could resign in lieu of termination in attempt to resolve the complaint. I shared in writing that the parties were forthcoming and candid until the end of the mediation, where

there was nothing else to discuss, because both parties would not come to an agreement. The mediator asked if there were any alternatives to resolve this complaint. As an attempt to resolve the complaint when asked, I stated resignation in lieu of termination.

10. Supervisor 1 said my participation was highly inappropriate, and I should be fully aware of the office's need to ensure integrity of the EEO complaint process. I did not actively participate in the mediation. If I had actively participated, I would have stated more than five words in a three-hour period, and I would have influenced a decision, which one was not made, and a decision was not on the table for review.

11. Supervisor 1 said "we" (management) have thought through the process very deliberately and cannot have EEO managers deviating from that process. I was not a manager, and I could not deviate from something that I was not made aware.

12. Supervisor 1 said if I had gone through her, my request would have been denied. I indicated that this statement was irrelevant. However, I informed Supervisor 1 that the next time this same situation comes up, I would let her know.

13. Supervisor 1 said if I was called to testify, she was not confident that I would not disclose any matter discussed. I care about my reputation

and my character; therefore, if called to testify, I would speak solely on my counseling.

I informed Supervisor 1 that the parties were allowed to bring an attorney or other representative to the mediation session. While it was not necessary to have an attorney or other representative in order to participate in the EEOC's mediation program, either party could choose to do so. The mediator decided what role the attorney or representative would play during the mediation. The mediator could ask that they provide advice and counsel, but not speak for a party. If a party planned to bring an attorney or other representative to the mediation session, he or she could discuss this with the mediator prior to the mediation session. My presence was discussed prior to the mediation with all parties aware of my position and agreed to. Neither party suffered harm for my attendance.

I filed an Administrative Grievance to the Executive Director and provided the above information, along with additional information as well. I informed the Executive Director that I had not committed an offense that warranted a Letter of Reprimand or any other type of punishment; therefore, I asked if he would dismiss this Letter of Reprimand with no further action. The Executive Director's decision was to resend the Letter of Reprimand, and issue me an oral counseling.

So, I received an oral counseling, a written counseling, a Letter of Reprimand, which was rescinded, and another oral counseling for attending a mediation when there was nothing in writing from the United States Customs and Border Protection (CBP) or EEOC that stated I could not attend. And when my customer, the person that I service requested my attendance.

I should not have been punished for something management did not tell me or provide written documentation regarding. The proper step to have taken was to inform me that we do not like our EEO counselors attending a mediation and state the reason(s). This should have been done sometime when I came on board to work—not after the action took place—if it was so important that disciplinary actions needed to take place. Because it happened after the fact, there should have only been a conversation between Supervisor 1 and me to make me aware of the information.

Complaint 3

Received Memorandum of Counseling for Tone in an Email

I counseled a case where the complainant in the case decided to go through the mediation process. I attempted for over a month to schedule this mediation between the complainant and a manager. Both parties were located in different states, and because of this, the complainant and the manager agreed to a telephonic mediation. This was the plan until an employee contacted me one day saying that she was the Coordinator and she wanted the complainant to come to her area for an in-person mediation, which was in a different state, and I already had an agreement for a telephonic mediation.

The Coordinator and I spoke about the complainant's EEO complaint, mediation, reasonable accommodation, and the EEO process for mediation. The Coordinator said that she was the person to speak with regarding this process to include scheduling. She asked me questions in different ways to get answers she was searching for. She insisted on providing questions to the complainant's physician regarding his disability. The Coordinator insisted on changing the mediation and having the complainant in person for the mediation. I guessed she was trying to take over the process. I did not like how the conversation was going, and I needed to move on to schedule the mediation. I asked the Coordinator if my supervisor could speak with her supervisor because I was having difficulties in scheduling the mediation. She was telling me how to do my job because she wanted an in-person mediation, so I told her to give the complainant a direct order if she wanted him in person because it was not up to me to agree to the type of mediation. I was only scheduling it.

The EEO Office timelines were per the Executive Director not the EEOC to show the number of mediations being conducted less than ninety days and different timeframes within the ninety days (thirty-to-sixty days) with no extensions for the Executive Director's benefit. Therefore, I was on a time schedule to get this mediation scheduled and completed, or I would have been counseled for not following procedures.

I was at the forty-ninth day, and it would have taken time to reschedule an in-person mediation. I first had to explain why I changed from a telephonic mediation to an in-person, having the complainant travel at his own expense for something that could happen over the telephone saving the complainant time and money. This way he could have returned to work instead of traveling back home.

The Coordinator decided to send me an email to talk about our conversations. She copied Supervisor 2, her supervisor, and counsel, who was a friend of the Executive Director. After reading the email, I disagreed with it, and I responded. I stated what the Coordinator reported, and I provided my response.

Counsel contacted the Executive Director and said that he was not going to "referee" a conversation between me and the Coordinator concerning the appropriateness of conducting the mediation in person or telephonically. Somehow, counsel's conversation with the Executive Director ended with a complaint filed against me for responding to incorrect information.

I received a Memorandum of Counseling for (1) the tone in my email for correcting the Coordinator, (2) a point by point email was inappropriate, (3) my method of refuting the Coordinator's email point by point was inappropriate, unprofessional and unnecessarily confrontational, (4) my tone throughout the email was curt and contrary to the quality of customer service I am expected to provide, (5) I should have known a complainant could not be given a direct order to appear in person for a mediation, as I was told the Agency could not compel an employee to attend a mediation session, and (6) that it was inappropriate for me to mention the timeline of the mediation process in my correspondence.

Supervisor 2 said I must ensure that my conduct and attitude during written and verbal correspondence with customers remained professional at all times and that failure to correct these issues would result in the initiation of formal disciplinary action, up to and including removal from my position with the federal service. Supervisor 2 said the Memorandum of Counseling was issued to correct my behavior and bring me into compliance with the policies and procedures of the United States CBP.

I informed Supervisor 2 that I had been very cordial, polite, and professional during the numerous telephone conversations I had, and that my concerns were servicing the complaint, timeliness, and moving the complaint. I also shared that based on my experience at CBP, my email was to protect myself, to provide written documentation whenever asked since the Coordinator copied her, her supervisor, and counsel. If I had not commented on what the Coordinator reported, the Coordinator's report would be true even if there were issues with it—and there were issues, even when I kept Supervisor 2 abreast of this situation from the beginning of my conversations with the Coordinator, the email, and that I wanted her to speak with the Coordinator's supervisor. Supervisor 2 was fully aware of my actions, and she had no concerns about me doing my job. I believe Supervisor 2 was instructed by the Executive Director to issue me a Letter of Counseling. Why else would she have done this when I had kept her abreast?

Intimidating and Threatening Telephone Call for Going to the Commissioner

The Executive Director sent an email to the staff regarding EEO Staff Realignment Notice. On the same date, I sent the Executive Director a response requesting that he reconsider his Realignment Notice due to the complaints I filed against the supervisors he wanted to supervise me and/or that I complained about. I filed a complaint against Supervisor 3 for contacting a management official prior to me receiving the anonymity form from a complainant who filed a complaint, and I was asked questions after the informal process was closed and after I filed a formal complaint. I said that I wanted to be treated as the other filers that "when a case is closed, it is closed." Supervisor 3 told Supervisor 8 to delete her questions that she prepared for me.

I requested Supervisor 6 to be my supervisor because she had done all she could to ensure I had a healthy work environment. I said that having Supervisor 3 and Assistant Director 2 at "arm's length" of me, I was a "sitting duck" for continuous harassment, a hostile work environment, and disciplinary actions similar to the ones I had received already. Supervisor 6's communication, listening, and supervisory skills had allowed me to be productive. I also shared that even though I had filed a complaint against the Executive Director, I hoped he felt the same way about me, as he noted in his email about customers "that we work together to achieve the best possible results for our customers; in my case, this was his employee.

Also, in my response, I said that I prayed that he found it to be in the best interest of the Agency, management, and me if I remain under Supervisor 6's supervision. The Executive Director respectfully denied my request.

I told the Executive Director thank you for taking time out of his busy schedule to address my request for reconsideration and for responding so quickly with a denial and no explanation. I also told him that I was concerned about my health, welfare, and performance of duty to include my service-connected disabilities, which were being aggravated by decisions and treatment of management while my chain of command is aware. Therefore, I informed him that I must take my concerns to the next level, his supervisor, the Commissioner.

I sent an email to the Commissioner and furnished a copy to the Executive Director. I introduced myself with my name, years in the military and the federal government, stated that I was a disabled veteran, and told him where I worked. I said that I was truly sorry for bringing my concerns to his level, but my concerns are important to my health and work production. I requested a meeting with him to speak about concerns in my workplace, especially being denied a reasonable and workable request. My chain of command (Executive Director (third-level supervisor), Supervisor 1 (second-level supervisor), and Supervisor 7 (first-level supervisor) were fully aware of this request. I asked if the Commissioner would please find time in his busy schedule to speak with me.

Instead of a response from the Commissioner, the Executive Director contacted me and said, "Based on your message to the Commissioner, are you requesting a reasonable accommodation under the Rehabilitation Act?" I responded:

"My email to the Commissioner is about my concerns regarding my health, welfare, and work production. It has nothing to do with requesting a reasonable accommodation under the Rehabilitation Act. If I was in a healthy work environment free of harassment there would be no concerns regarding my health, welfare, and work production."

The Executive Director informed me that to his knowledge, no United States CBP staff member engaged in any action with regard to me that could reasonably be considered harassing by any standard. He asked that I allow him to better understand my current allegation, and he asked me to identify the individual or individuals who subjected me to harassment and the specific harassing actions that were taken against me. He said upon receipt of my response, he would review the facts and take all action necessary to address my concerns if my allegations were substantiated.

I responded to the Executive Director and said that I was complex about his statement and I disagreed with his statement. I said he was aware of the harassment and hostile work environment and the individuals. Since I had many incidents to compile, I needed time to prepare and submit. Matters that had not been resolved were current matters until they were resolved.

I informed the Executive Director that I believed that because he was involved in my incidents and had allowed them to occur and continue, he was not the appropriate person to look into the matter and take action. However, I informed the Executive Director that since he said he would review the facts and take all action necessary to address my concerns, if my allegations were substantiated, that I would provide him the information as requested, and I would like to have a copy of the findings.

Based on the way we operated, I had to keep my chain of command abreast of my hours. Supervisor 7 (first-level supervisor) and Supervisor 3 (second-level supervisor) were furnished copies of all emails.

I was looking for a better work environment; one free from harassment. Instead, I received a telephone call from the Executive Director, which was unusual. There was one other telephone call he made to me. He called me when I claimed harassment on Supervisor 1. The Executive Director stated that he knew Supervisor 1, and he said she would not do what I said and he told me that I did not complete the Outside Employment Application. I thought I had better write down the conversation because there was no need for him to contact me when I was working on what he requested in writing.

The Executive Director asked me why I contacted the Commissioner. He stated that the Commissioner did not make decisions about the reconstruction of the office. He asked if I understood that the Commissioner could not help me because he did not make decisions regarding the reconstruction of our office. I informed the Executive Director that the information he had requested, I would provide to him. The Executive Director asked me over and over why I contacted the Commissioner. He was fully aware because I copied him on the email I sent to the Commissioner, so I could not understand this conversation.

The Executive Director said it was not clearly stated why I contacted the Commissioner. He asked me over and over for me to give him a reason. I asked if I could get back with him, and the Executive Director said no. I informed the Executive Director that I was not feeling well, and again I asked if I could get back with him; he said no and asked for an answer right then. Again, I told the Executive Director that I was not feeling well and asked if I could get back with him. He said no and again asked for me to tell him right then.

I asked the Executive Director if he was forcing me to tell him now, and he said he was not forcing me, but he wanted the answer now. The Executive Director said the reconstruction was done and that it had nothing to do with my situation. He said that he knew I was stressed about my complaint because filing complaints is stressful. He continued by stating that no one had done anything that day or the day before to me that he was aware of. He asked why I sent an email to Supervisor 7, because he was two levels below him and did not need to know. The Executive Director told me that Supervisor 7 was a new employee and had no information about me.

The Executive Director asked what happened to me, and I told him that I would like to put it in writing as he requested. He asked me again for the reason right then. I told him again that I was not feeling well, and asked if I could tell him later. He said no. I further said that I was concerned about my health and was not feeling well and asked to please provide the information later. The Executive Director denied me and said I was to provide it then. I said again that I was not feeling well and if I could get back with him, and he denied me.

He commented that I mentioned something about my health, and in my email that I requested reasonable accommodation. I told the Executive Director that I did not say that I was requesting reasonable accommodation in my email. The Executive Director told me to watch my tone and asked me if I was refusing to answer his question. I said that I was not refusing to answer his question, I would just rather put it in writing as requested. He denied me and said for me to answer his question "now." He said if I did not answer his question, it would be considered as refusal. The Executive Director said he had addressed my issues, no one had any problems with me, there was no performance or conduct issue, and my issues were out of context. The Executive Director went on to say that he knew nothing about someone doing something to me today or a few days ago, and he wanted me to answer his question. I said I was not feeling well and asked if I could get back with him, and he said no. You will answer my question. I was silent. The Executive Director said, "Penny, Penny, if you do not answer me, I will assume you hung up on me and disciplinary action will be taken." I passed out.

When I came to, I contacted the Veterans Administration Medical Center, sent an email to the Executive Director and copied Supervisor 7 on the email to say that I was going to the hospital because I passed out during my conversation with him (Executive Director). I contacted Supervisor 2 and told her what happened. She contacted the Director, Baltimore Field Operations because I was working on a different floor from his office. I noticed I had a lump on my forehead, and I was in pain. The Director, Baltimore Field Operations, his staff members, and security came to my office, saw me shaking, and asked me what happened. As I stated what happened, I passed out again, and a staff member picked me up off the floor.

When I came to, I had bruises on my legs, a lump on the other side of my head, and my body was aching. The paramedics were called. Once they got to my office, they asked me what happened. As I was telling them, I passed out again. The paramedics took me to the emergency room.

This was brought on by being harassed, intimidated, threatened, and coerced by the Executive Director during the telephone conversation. There was an Internal Affairs investigation on the incident. It is my understanding that the Executive Director requested this investigation. Internal Affairs is within the DHS. The question that I was asked over and over by the investigator if I taped the conversation. I said no that I wrote down the conversation as it was happening. I had to show my handwritten notes of the conversation. Had I taped the conversation without the Executive Director's approval, I would have been guilty of an illegal act of taping the conversation, and what the Executive Director did to me would have been a dead issue.

I emailed the Commissioner again and said that I regret this second email regarding my concerns about the EEO Office, but I wanted to say since the first email, the Executive Director contacted me two times by email and telephone. When he contacted me by telephone, he harassed, intimidated, threatened and coerced me to the point that I became physically ill and passed out. Once the Baltimore Field Operations Director found out that I passed out, he, the Assistant Director of Field Operations, CBP Officers, civilian employees, security, and the paramedics came to my office where I passed out two more times, and I required immediate hospitalization. I informed the Commissioner that the medical professional found that I suffered an anxiety attack brought on by the Executive Director's hostile and aggressive behavior on the telephone. I also mentioned that this incident would be part of my ongoing complaint against the Executive Director and his managers.

I went on to say that I was bringing this matter to his attention because I was not able to resolve it at the lowest possible level. I said that there needed to be an intervention, not only for myself, but for other EEO specialists that feel reprisal for speaking out. A review of the EEO Office will disclose that my situation is not isolated or unique, and I am not the only victim of this type of treatment. I told the Commissioner that I was seeking his help to have a safer and healthier work environment for the employees and myself; especially after reviewing the Safety Stand Down video the DHS

Secretary asked all employees to view. I thanked the Commissioner in advance and asked that I have no contact with the Executive Director to avoid further retaliation and health issues. I received no response.

I sent an email to DHS Secretary regarding my hostile work environment, my injuries, and requested assistance. I received no response.

What I did receive, was a letter from Supervisor 7 regarding my emails to the Commissioner and the DHS Secretary. He said that my emails to the Commissioner and the DHS Secretary were unprofessional, and it was completely inappropriate to use language like "mentally raped." Neither the Commissioner nor the Secretary was the appropriate party to resolve my allegations or my request for reassignment, and I should not have contacted them.

Therefore, until further notice Supervisor 7 said that he was my immediate supervisor, and he should be the first person notified in my chain of command should I need to discuss work-related concerns. Supervisor 7 gave me a direct order stating that any and all matters affecting my working conditions and/or conditions of employment must be addressed through my chain of command. He continued to say that this was a direct order to cease and desist sending emails to the Commissioner or the Secretary. I went through my chain of command and Supervisor 7 was aware.

I filed a Workers' Compensation Claim for the injuries I sustained while working. The Executive Director challenged it, stating that my condition was not a result of a work-related injury. I was at work at my desk working when the Executive Director contacted me. Workers' Compensation accepted the claim for the physical head contusion injury, but not for sustained stress headaches due to an employment related injury, based on the fact that I struck my forehead on my desk and phone after I fainted, which would be considered a contributing, intervening employment hazard.

What the Executive Director did not know was that I knew when he got off the telephone with me, he walked out of his office and made the comment, "I did not do that." He did not realize his comment was heard. Not until the employee who heard about what happened to me and the time that it happened put two and two together and realized the comment the Executive Director stated was about me. The employee then notified me. I never mentioned this for fear that something might happen to the employee.

I filed a complaint with the Office of Special Counsel. This office is also within DHS. The Office of Special Counsel stated their review of my complaint of retaliation for whistleblowing, arbitrary and capricious withholding Freedom of Information Act, improperly denied my Administrative Grievance and part of Workers' Compensation claim, and violating my rights in providing the cease and desist order for utilizing my chain of command, found that the only issue that they could address was the cease and desist order. The Office of Special Counsel contacted the Executive Director and stated that the cease and desist order must be rescinded.

After reviewing the letter, I responded to the Office of Special Counsel. I expressed how I was treated. I expressed how it was not right to slap a manager on the hand for violating my rights in providing the cease and desist order for utilizing my chain of command.

I expressed providing management with a notice to correct the cease and desist order when the order no longer existed was no punishment at all in comparison to what I had suffered for seven years under the supervision of the Executive Director, his managers, and supervisors. I continued by sharing that when there is a personal intent to cause harm to an employee when you are a manager and get a slap on the hand is unbelievable. In this situation, the Executive Director should have been held accountable and responsible for his actions or inactions of having someone else do his "dirty work" to not link him to the situation.

I concluded by sharing that I understood how this process worked; it is not for the employee, because I did not get justice. It is so sorry to say that my tax-paying dollars encourage this type of behavior with no "proper" action taken."

I got a new supervisor, Supervisor 9, and I emailed him to say that I understood that he was not my supervisor at the time, and he did not want to get involved, but because he is my supervisor now, he is involved. I informed Supervisor 9 that I wished to move forward without thinking about what the managers and supervisors in this office had done to me during the past seven years, but I told him I was damaged goods. I would do my job, but I could not forget what they had done to me and what might happen in the future as long as I was assigned to the same office. Maybe if management and supervisors had taken responsibility for their actions and been held accountable, it might have been easier to move forward and put them behind me without looking over my shoulder.

Complaint 5

Opened a Closed Complaint When the Notice of Right to File Was Issued

I filed an informal complaint, which consisted of contacting an EEO specialist within forty-five days of the date of the alleged discriminatory act or within forty-five days of the effective date of the personnel or employment action. Once you make contact, your issue is assigned a counselor, and that counselor has thirty days to counsel the complaint and ninety days for mediation that includes either settlement or providing the Notice of Right to File a Formal Complaint.

I requested mediation in a case I submitted. This particular complaint was pending mediation. I sent Counselor 1 an email saying that I had cooperated throughout the process, but the unidentified management official whom I believe to be Supervisor 1 continued to harass me throughout this process. The supervisor retaliated against me, continued to aggravate my medical conditions, and prevented me from moving forward with my cases. Therefore, I informed Counselor 1 that it would be in the best interest of the agency and myself, in protecting my health and career, that I move my first complaint in counseling to receive the Final Interview and the Notice of Right to File a Formal Complaint. I asked Counselor 1 to send me the Notice of Right to File a Formal Complaint to my home email address and furnish a copy to my work email address.

I moved to have my second complaint go through the informal process to obtain a case number. I asked Counselor 1 to let me know when a "spin off" complaint would be conducted." I received the Final Interview and the Notice of Rights to File on the first complaint. Counselor 1 said he would provide me with a case number for the second complaint and move that complaint forward through the informal complaint process. I provided Counselor 1 with the counseling forms, and I requested mediation.

While in EEO training, I asked Counselor 1 if he had a case number for my second complaint, and he stated that he had to amend my Notice of Right to File in the informal process to add the second complaint. He asked if I had received that email, and I said no, that was why I was asking for the case number for the filed complaint. What happened was that Supervisor 1 directed Counselor 1 to retract the Notice of Right to File and amend the first complaint with the second complaint so it will be one complaint. I was denied "proper" processing of my informal complaint. The policies state the following:

1. CFR 1614.106(d), Individual Complaints, "A complainant may amend a complaint at any time prior to the conclusion of the investigation to include issues or <u>claims</u> like or related

to those raised in the complaint." I was denied "proper" processing of my informal complaint.

2. CFR 1614.106(e), Individual Complaints, "The agency shall acknowledge receipt of a complaint in the formal process or an amendment to a complaint in writing and inform the complainant of the date on which the complaint or amendment was filed." I was denied "proper" processing of my informal complaint.

3. MD110, EEO Pre-Complaint Processing
    a. "Advise the aggrieved individual about the EEO complaint process."
    b. "Determine the claim(s) and basis(es) raised by the aggrieved individual."
    c. "Conduct a limited inquiry during the initial interview with the aggrieved individual."
    d. "Seek a resolution of the dispute at the lowest possible level."
    e. "Advise the aggrieved individual of his/her right to file a formal discrimination complaint."
    f. "Prepare a report sufficient to document that the EEO Counselor undertook the required counseling actions."
    g. "Advise the aggrieved person that their identity will not be revealed unless the aggrieved person authorizes them to reveal it or they file a formal complaint with the agency."

There is no language in this that speaks about counselors amending complaints. I was denied "proper" processing of my informal complaint.

4. The U.S. Equal Employment Opportunity Commission has developed a guide for EEO counseling that agencies may use in developing or refining their own procedures.

5. The EEO Office Directions for Completion for documenting and Tracking Informal EEO Contacts is to ensure that allegations are processed in compliance with applicable laws, regulations, executive orders and policies. EEO contact cases may require a significant amount of time and attention and should be tracked. The EEO Office policy under the Directions for Completion Checklist, Intake of Informal EEO Complaints, Assignment Log states that it "will be utilized to track and notify" EEO "staff members of counseling assignments." When a complainant requests to file an informal complaint, the case is inputted in the complaint system. I was denied "proper" processing of my informal complaint.

6. The EEO Office procedure is to submit the information into the Complaint System within two working days. I submitted the second complaint, and it was never inputted in the system accordingly. I was denied "proper" processing of my informal complaint.

7. At the EEO conference, Supervisor 3 informed us once a person elected to file an informal complaint, the information goes into the Complaint System within two days. I was denied "proper" processing of my informal complaint.

8. At the EEO conference, Supervisor 3 informed us that cases are not amended in the informal

process. They are amended in the formal process. She also informed us that you cannot open a Notice of Right to File after the case was closed to amend it with a new complaint. I was denied "proper" processing of my informal complaint.

9. I agreed to enter into mediation in good faith, and I was denied "proper" processing of my informal complaint.

10. The amended Notice of Right to File did not state my claim of continuous harassment resulting in a hostile work environment. The write-up was not complete to what I stated in my written informal complaint. Counselor 1 mentioned early on in the amended Notice of Right to File a supervisor title, yet he did not state the Commissioner's title in this claim. I was denied "proper" processing of my informal complaint.

11. According to MD110, EEO Pre-Complaint Processing, "If informal resolution is not possible, the EEO Counselor must hold a final interview with the aggrieved person and issue the Notice of Right to File a Discrimination Complaint." I did not receive the Final Interview through the informal process. I was denied "proper" processing of my informal complaint.

12. I requested to send the complaint through the informal process. I was denied "proper" processing of my informal complaint.

13. At the EEO conference, the Executive Director informed his employees to communicate, resolve complaints, have integrity, and provide

customer service. I was denied all this in the processing of my informal complaint.

I requested that Counselor 1 retract the amended Notice of Right to File and allow my informal complaint to go through the informal process as regulation and procedures state and as the EEO Office has done for other similar situated complainants. The amended Notice of Right to File was never retracted.

Complaint 6

Delayed Outside Employment Application

I submitted a Request to Engage in Outside Employment to Supervisor 7 with follow ups every month for four months. Since four months had passed, and I had not received the approval for my application, I sent an email to Supervisor 3 to see if she was aware of my request. Later, I received a letter from Supervisor 3, which a legal opinion was provided for me to sign a document with guidelines from the Standards of Ethical Conduct for Employees of the Executive Branch.

I had submitted this request every year, and it had never taken this long, and I did not have to sign a legal opinion with guidelines from the Standards of Ethical Conduct for Employees of the Executive Branch.

Complaint 7

Set Up for Failure

In this particular situation, I was on leave. When I returned from leave, I checked my email and noticed a request titled EEO Document Request Not Reasonable Accommodation. Since this was not a reasonable accommodation request, I continued checking my emails. I found out six days later that it was a reasonable accommodation request—these requests are time sensitive. If I did not process a reasonable accommodation request within the timeframe allowed then I would receive some type of disciplinary action, so I was concerned.

I sent an email to Supervisor 5 because he was the supervisor for the area, I was responsible for, and I furnished a copy to Supervisor 3 and Supervisor 7, about receiving the reasonable accommodation request six days into the process. I asked to allow me to express myself and to be "frank" without fear of disciplinary action. I voiced my concerns and frustrations of being set up for failure and being on hyper-alert to defend myself. I also said that I just wanted to do my job without fear of action taken against me for someone else's short falls. Now, I have to waste time to address this issue to protect myself, I told them. I wanted to know why I received the request when I was on leave instead of it being assigned to another facilitator. I wanted to know why Supervisor 5 issued the request forms to start the process when it was the facilitator's job. I wanted to know why Supervisor 5 sent me an email saying it was not a reasonable accommodation request when he knew it was because he provided the forms. I wanted to know if I would be penalized for the days lost.

I believe Supervisor 7 attempted to come to Supervisor 5's defense to say, not in these exact words but similar, that supervisors have a lot on their plate, and I should understand as being a manager in the past. My response was that no matter what the circumstances were, I was flexible and could juggle the work, but I always took care of my employees whether military or civilian. Unlike here, where management wanted to find fault to punish unless it was someone he or she favors.

Supervisor 7 informed me that this problem would be resolved with the new EEO specialists being trained. If we hired people with EEO experience, they would be able to do the job immediately; especially at the grade level they were being hired. Since they were not trained and experienced EEO specialists, they were unable to assist, which overburdened the trained and experienced EEO specialists. Even after training, by not having experience as an EEO specialist, they still needed time.

This was not fair to us EEO specialists because we had been asking for help and had not received it, receiving only mismanagement of people and distribution of work. No one had asked us trained and experienced EEO specialists what would work for us to lessen the burden, the amount of changes, for us to work smartly, and produce a great product.

Do you see how we went from my concerns of processing a six-day old request that is time sensitive to supervisors having a lot on their plate to hiring more EEO specialists? My concerns were not addressed. I lost six days in processing the request and had to complete it within the timeframe of completing a reasonable accommodation request, or I would have received some type of disciplinary action.

Complaint 8

Denied 4/10
Work Schedule

I requested to work a 4/10 shift, work four ten-hour days, to have less time at work. Supervisor 7 denied my request stating that it applied to union members. I informed him what the policy stated, which was that it was for all employees as long as the supervisor approved it based on the workload. Deputy Director 1 was assigned to the EEO Office. Since she came from the Labor and Employees Relations Office and knew the policy, I requested a 4/10 shift from her, and she approved it. Not only did she approve a 4/10 shift, she allowed me to work from six in the morning to four thirty in the afternoon, which gave me at least two hours to do my job before other employees of the EEO Office came to work.

Complaint 9

Opened a Closed Report of Investigation Where a Hearing Was Requested

The Director, Baltimore Field Operations had a meeting with an employee from his office and me, as an EEO Counselor, to find out if his employee was speaking with me without requesting official time. When I said the employee did speak with me, the employee called me a liar. The Director, Baltimore Field Operations asked me to leave the room. Among other things and this incident, the employee was provided with a Letter of Reprimand. She requested counseling, but from another counselor.

The employee spoke with Counselor 4 about the meeting; the employee called me a liar and stated that I could not be trusted, along with comments about other work-related issues, because the employee received a Letter of Reprimand. Counselor 4 informed the employee to send the Executive Director an email that included the statements she made about me.

The normal process when a complainant files a complaint against an EEO specialist or a counselor is for the counselor to notify his or her chain of command. In this situation, it was Supervisor 5 and the next level, Supervisor 1. The supervisor would request a spin off complaint to initiate an inquiry into the matter by another EEO specialist. Instead, Counselor 4 informed the complainant to send an email to the Executive Director, our third-level supervisor. The Executive Director took the employee's statements that I was a liar and could not be trusted, had Supervisor 4, the Formal Complaint supervisor opened my four-month old closed Report of Investigation when I requested an EEOC Hearing to input the statements to discredit my character for complaints I filed against him.

This information was irrelevant to the case. It was new information that was not investigated in the EEO process to find if there were any merits, investigation was already conducted in the matter, and it was closed. I did not receive "proper" notification in the cover letter when I was notified the reason the Report of Investigation was revised and what was the revision. In addition, I was not afforded due process to provide a statement to any of my chain of command prior to the Executive Director having the false statements inputted in my closed Report of Investigation to be reviewed at the hearing.

Supervisor 5 informed me the case the employee brought against me was completed and closed with no action taken. Meaning, there were no findings of the employee allegation against me.

What the Executive Director did was illegal to have his employee, Supervisor 4, open a four-month-old closed Report of Investigation when the case was already at EEOC pending a hearing to revise it with the false statements from the employee about me. The Executive Director knew I had requested a hearing in this case, and when you request a hearing, any and all information is brought up in the hearing process. Had he waited, he would have found there was no merit to the complainant's false statements against me, and as this was the case, there was no information to input. If the Executive Director had spoken with me prior to having the information inputted, he would have known the statements were false or at least received information to make that determination. However, the Executive Director had an alternative motive in intentionally sliding that piece of information into my closed Report of Investigation to discredit me when the file was reviewed at the hearing. This was a direct and personal attack on my character for filing complaints against him, and it was an integrity issue.

As a remedy, I requested the false statements the Executive Director inputted into my close Report of Investigation removed from the Report of Investigation, and I was denied.

I sent an email to the Joint Intake Center. This center serves as the "clearinghouse" for receiving, processing, and tracking of allegations of misconduct involving personnel and contractors employed by CBP. The Joint Intake Center provides CBP with a centralized and uniform system for processing reports of alleged misconduct. All reports of misconduct were coordinated with the DHS Office of Inspector General and referred to the appropriate office for investigation, fact-finding, or immediate management action.

The Joint Intake Center policy on reporting misconduct states "that reports of alleged misconduct may not result in any immediate action or overt signs of activity. Do not assume a lack of visible activity means your report has been ignored or met with indifference. All reports, including those submitted anonymously, receive prompt and complete attention. Employees are subject to disciplinary action for failing to report allegations of misconduct. Allegations of misconduct are to be immediately reported"

The email that I sent to the Joint Intake Center was a request to file a complaint against the Executive Director for intentional wrongdoing, deliberate violation of standard, improper behavior, and bad management practice. The Executive Director used his position and authority to circumvent the administrative process to his advantage for personal gain and failing to follow procedures of the process to discredit me for the many complaints I filed against him. I informed the Joint Intake Center that this was not an EEO complaint, it was not a complaint against the process, but a complaint against the Executive Director's action in abusing his position and authority.

Complaint 10

Received a Letter of Reprimand for Providing Case Number to a Counselor per Her Request

I was the Receiving Official filling in for a coworker. As the Receiving Official, I checked the responsibilities for processing complaints in our operating procedures because they change. It states to process contacts and requests for informal EEO counseling. As the Receiving Official, I inputted my information in the database as requested, I sent an acknowledgement email, and an email to Supervisor 5 for assignment. Supervisor 5 contacted me, and we had a discussion about inputting my complaint.

I informed Supervisor 5 that I did not know that I could not input my own complaint as the Receiving Official with the basic information: name, title, series, grade, office location, and the allegation. As the Receiving Official, it states to process complaints, and I had a complaint, and I processed it as the Receiving Official in the performance of my duties. I saw nothing in writing that said otherwise. Supervisor 5 told me that "we do not do that," and I acknowledged it.

This situation had never been discussed verbally or in writing to know not to process your complaint as the Receiving Official. You act on the Standard Operating Procedures step-by-step written documentation. The procedures state what to do in every aspect of your responsibilities until a written document or a verbal statement is made. The only thing that I provided was my information, which had to be verified by the Assigning Official. This was an error that I was informed after the fact by Supervisor 5, and it had not happened again.

As a supervisor, this was the correct action to take, talk to me and make me aware, not to provide punishment for something I did not know — especially with the number of complaints that I filed. My chain of command should have made that very clear to me since I had filed complaints knowing I would be the Receiving Official.

I received a Letter of Instruction from Supervisor 1 that stated she received allegations that I had used the Complaint System for personal purposes; specifically, for the purpose of creating my own EEO complaint, and accessing records on my previous complaints unrelated to my official duties, and that I was the subject of an allegation of misconduct, and to give me a direct order that if I have engaged in the conduct described, I must immediately cease and desist from such conduct. Supervisor 1 gave me a cease and desist from accessing all CBP computer and information systems, including the Complaint System for personal reasons unrelated to my official duties.

A review of all of the facts and circumstances surrounding the allegations were completed. Supervisor 1 informed me that I would have an opportunity to respond to any subsequent administrative action. She said that she had not formed an opinion regarding the current allegations, and she wanted me to understand that this Letter of Instruction was not disciplinary in nature, and it would not become a matter of record in my official personnel folder.

Supervisor 1 denied me the use to work on my complaints using CBP computers and information systems until Counselor 2 informed her that it was illegal to deny me and no other employees. Supervisor 1 revised the Letter of Instructions informing me that I may use the CBP telephone, computer, printer, copier, or fax and participate in my scheduled mediation session in order to continue processing my EEO complaint. I informed Deputy Director 1 what happened. Her response was that I was not denied for a long time. Overlooking the bottom line of being denied, which was illegal.

Months later, I was under an Internal Affairs investigation for misconduct. I recall I was in my office, one of the investigators came to get me to go into another office to ask me questions. When I walked in the room, there were three chairs: one in the middle, which was my chair, and the other two chairs were in front of me, one on each side. The room was hot, and the men were tall and big in size to give an intimidating appearance. I felt like I was being interrogated based on how the questions were asked; it was as if I had committed a crime. This was in contrast to another time that I was investigated, which was totally different.

You have to ask yourself, what is misconduct? In Wikipedia Encyclopedia, misconduct is "a legal term meaning a wrongful, improper, or unlawful conduct motivated by premeditated or intentional purpose". "Misconduct in the workplace generally falls under two categories. Minor misconduct is seen as unacceptable but is not a criminal offense (e.g. being late). Gross misconduct can lead to dismissal, (e.g. stealing or sexual harassment)."

Supervisor 1 attempted to paint a picture that my conduct was illegal and intentionally against policy. There was no misconduct. I did not do anything illegally, intentionally, or against policy. It was an error that was corrected by Supervisor 5. I should not have been penalized, especially, when Supervisor 1, in the same instruction, denied me access to all CBP computer and information systems when other employees used it for their complaints. She said that her actions were in error; she apologized, and retracted her statement after she was notified by Counselor 2 on my case that her actions were illegal.

Supervisor 1's actions toward me were retaliation against me for filing so many complaints against her. Supervisor 5 and I had the conversation, Supervisor 1 did not ask me any questions, and instead she issued an investigation on misconduct. Again, not until Counselor 2 informed Supervisor 1 that she was having difficulties in processing my complaint because of her statement in the Letter of Instruction, and that she could not deny me access to work on my complaints, as other employees were allowed to do so, the letter was changed.

Supervisor 8 contacted me via telephone to inform me that I would be receiving a Letter of Reprimand. In that conversation, she expressed that if I had questions I should speak with the Labor and Employee Relations point of contact. She also made the same statement to contact a Labor and Employee Relations point of contact in her cover letter along with stating if I had any questions about the contents of her letter or my rights to contact the Labor and Employee Relations point of contact.

When I received the letter, I reviewed it, and concluded that I did not violate any laws, regulations, or policies because it was not stated, and my punishment would have been more severe—as in removal from the position of EEO specialist. What was stated were incorrect or incomplete statements to punish me: accessing the contact log, insubordination, tracking my personal complaints, statements of "as you know" and "should have known," and the reason to issue the letter was to correct my misconduct and deter me from engaging in future acts of misconduct. At no time prior to the letter did management speak with me, but management drew a conclusion based on other employee statements and an investigative report that I never received and was never spoken to about.

Let's look at the allegations in the Letter of Reprimand and the facts to show when you file complaints against a supervisor and/or manager some of the consequences you will encounter for standing up and speaking out.

Allegation: I accessed the Contact Log in Complaint System to see who was assigned to my case and asked Assistant Director 1 to change my counselor. I requested this change before I was formally notified via email of my assigned counselor.

Fact: I did not access the Contact Log to see who was assigned to my case. In the performance of my duties as a Counselor inputting a complaint into the Complaint System, you see complaints that all of us are assigned to and the complainant's name. Supervisor 5 went into Complaint System and changed information that I inputted regarding him without telling me. I was scheduled to brief Supervisor 1 and Acting Supervisor. I informed them both, but no Internal Affair investigation was conducted, as it was in my case, because no one from Internal Affairs spoke with me. Supervisor 5 changed information about him for personal reasons, and I added my complaint in an official capacity as the Receiving Official and turned it over to the Assigning Official. I received a Letter of Instruction, verbal counseling, Internal Affairs investigation, and a Letter of Reprimand. Supervisor 5 received nothing.

Allegation: Assistant Director 1 told me to do a verbal interview like any other complaint.

Fact: Assistant Director 1 did not tell me as in giving me an order to have a verbal interview. The conversation went like this in an email:

> Assistant Director 1, I guess I should have told you who has been involved in my previous complaints to help with selecting someone. Counselor 2 was another person that I had issues with counseling one of my complaints. I will not ask to select someone else, because you did already. What I will say is that the initial interview will be in writing to prevent situation

that occurred in the past to happen this time. What I informed the counselor during the initial interview was not the same in the Counselor's Report: a report with the details of the complaint. Assistant Director 1 suggested I submit something in writing summarizing everything, and that a verbal interview should be conducted like we would do in any informal complaint. The word "should be" is not telling me.

My response was the Complaint System had a summary of my concern. I understand that a verbal interview should be conducted like we do in any informal complaint under normal circumstances, but this was not one. I told Assistant Director 1 that I wanted to go through traditional counseling, receive my Notice of Right to File, have this complaint consolidated with my pending complaints at hearing, and file a formal complaint.

When Counselor 2 contacted me, we had a verbal counseling wherein I informed her that I wanted to resolve all of my complaints. I also spoke with the Assistant Director 1 regarding my complaints after Counselor 2 departed the EEO Office.

I recall the last time I was the Receiving Official: a complainant contacted me because she was upset with Assistant Director 1 and wanted to file a complaint against him for speaking with management about her conversation. The complainant thought the conversation was confidential because she did not sign an Authorization to Reveal her Identity, and she did not want management to know. The EEO Office had a policy of Preventing the Unauthorized Disclosure of Complainant's Identity During Informal Counseling, giving the right of an aggrieved person to remain anonymous during the informal EEO counseling process. This act was against a written policy. I informed Supervisor 8, and she stated that she guessed a spin off complaint would be done. No one contacted me to ask me questions regarding this matter.

Allegation: I accessed the Complaint System to track all of my personal complaints for the purpose of giving the information to Counselor 2, my assigned counselor.

Fact: I did not access the Complaint System to track all of my personal complaints. Counselor 2 asked me to verify my six complaints via email. I checked my records at home and they were not the same as what she provided; therefore, I went into the Complaint System to get the case numbers for verification to compare with what I had to report back to her. I did not add or delete information from my cases. Going into my complaints was related to my official duties to verify information for Counselor 2. For example: Supervisor 9 did a spin off complaint on me, he requested information over and over, and I provided the information over and over. He had me on the telephone after the end of my work day on hold while he searched for my documents and said that he found them. Supervisor 9 started asking personal questions and making me feel like I was being interrogated. Therefore, I stated that I would like to speak with my attorney. Supervisor 9 and I both agreed that I would notify Supervisor 1. Instead, he contacted

Supervisor 1 and told her that I would not provide the information requested. Supervisor 1 contacted me and gave me a direct order to provide Supervisor 9 with the information without a chance to respond.

Rules of Behavior: Do not retrieve information for someone who does not have the authority to access the information. Only give information to personnel who have access authority and have a need to know for their job. Counselor 2 had access authority, the authority to access the information, and a need to know.

Allegation: If I wish to initiate an EEO complaint, the appropriate method is to either contact a Receiving Official other than myself.

Fact: According to the standard procedures, Receiving Official duties does not state the "appropriate method" to initiate an EEO complaint by the person being the Receiving Official, and no management official brought it to my attention knowing how many complaints I filed and my duties until after the fact.

Allegation: The Complaint System is for the purpose of performing your official duties. Accessing the Complaint System for any reason other than to perform your official duties is prohibited. The required annual CBP Rules of Behavior training makes it clear that CBP systems are to be used for official duties only.

Fact: Accessing the Complaint System was in my official duty as the Receiving Official to input the complaint and provide Counselor 2 with information per her request as the counselor. With my history in the EEO Office in filing complaints against management, I cannot know something until it is stated in writing or verbal, and it was not until after the fact. I recall receiving a Letter of Reprimand by Supervisor 1 for attending a mediation when EEOC regulations state I can as long as I do not speak on behalf of the person. The EEO Office did not have a policy in place that stated otherwise, and Supervisor 1 did not tell me until after the fact when I informed her that Director, Baltimore Field Operations, the customer I service, requested my attendance. She gave me a Letter of Reprimand for something I did not know.

CBP policy states an employee has limited use to CBP information system for personal use. The Complaint System provides the ability to create, track, manage, and report on EEO complaint cases. Unlike going into secure systems.

Allegation: I am issuing you this Letter of Reprimand with the goal to correct your misconduct and to deter you from engaging in future acts of misconduct.

Fact: This Letter of Reprimand did not correct my misconduct nor deter me from engaging in future acts of misconduct because I was not involved in misconduct. Once I became aware by Supervisor 5 that Receiving Officials do not input their own complaints, is when no further action was taken. It had nothing to do with a misconduct issue. It is taking proper action to inform me that we do not input our own complaints as the Receiving Official instead of taking disciplinary action for management failing to tell me. For example: when I received verbal counseling, written counseling, Letter of Reprimand downgraded to a verbal written counseling for attending mediation when the EEOC regulations state I can if management requests, which Director, Baltimore Field Operations did, and when the EEO Office had no written or verbally-stated policy until after the fact.

I requested the Letter of Reprimand be rescinded and removed from my Official Personnel File. There was no misconduct, inappropriate use or behavior, insubordination, illegal or wrongful act, or a security violation or breach on my part. CBP policy covers its employees to use CBP Information System for official, and a limited amount of personal, use. I did not remove or change information in the system. My action was not intentional, and I had no knowledge base. There was no written policy, guidelines, or standard operating procedures that a Receiving Official who input complaints cannot input their own complaint. I acted on what the standard procedures stated and what Counselor 2 requested out of fear of what would happen if I did not get the information.

It is CBP policy to maintain a climate of openness in which an employee can feel free to express concerns and dissatisfactions and to use the grievance system for their resolution. It is also CBP policy to afford covered employees' ample opportunity to obtain consideration of issues concerning matters personally affecting them, which are subject to management control. Administrative Grievance is not the same as a Union Grievance. I can file an Administrative Grievance but not a Union Grievance because of my position as an EEO Specialist.

I contacted the Labor Employee Relations point of contact via email regarding the content of the letter and my rights to receive information, and I provided the following questions.

1. Do my rights include a conversation with my supervisor on the Letter of Reprimand prior to issuing it? If not, why not?
2. Do my rights include an oral or written reconsideration of the Letter of Reprimand? If not, why not?
3. Do my rights include an appeal to the Executive Director on the Letter of Reprimand? If no, why not?
4. Please provide a copy of the information that supported the decision of a Letter of Reprimand.
5. Please provide a copy of the Internal Affairs investigation that provided the finding of their investigation that was used in the decision to issue a Letter of Reprimand.
6. Please provide a copy of the policy, regulation, or law that governs the violation I committed.
7. Please provide a copy of the evidence held against me.
8. Please let me know what form of misconduct I committed while working in an official capacity as the Receiving Official.
9. Who was the person(s) that made the recommendation for the Letter of Reprimand?
10. Was my statement taken into consideration in consulting with management?

11. Was there a range of penalties provided to management? If so, what were they?
12. Please provide the names that were involved in the discussion in making the decision to give me a Letter of Reprimand?
13. Please provide any and all information and documents used to come to the decision of issuing me Letter of Reprimand?

After many attempts to contact the Labor and Employee Relations point of contact Supervisor 8 provided with no response to answer my questions, I reached out to her supervisor. I asked the supervisor to answer the thirteen questions with six additional questions so I could make a decision whether to file an Administrative Grievance or not. The additional six questions were:

1. Why was this letter issued when the information is taken out of context, is incomplete, and it provides a false account of what happened?
2. How can you provide a Letter of Reprimand on "As you know" and/or "as you should have known" instead of facts of actually knowing?
3. What is the purpose of the Complaint System?
4. Is the Complaint System the same as secure systems? If so, how come the same level of security or disclosure is not stated when you open the Complaint System?
5. Why was there a conversation with all parties involved in this Letter, and Supervisor 8 who issued the Letter to me did not speak with me? When you do not get the information from the

source, it can be distorted, which it has been in this case.

6. What action did Labor and Employee Relations recommend to Supervisor 8 or any other EEO representative in this matter?

The supervisor did not answer all my questions. Specifically, she did not answer the last six questions, and she informed Supervisor 3. The other thirteen questions, she answered with a politically correct statement, and she provided no documents per my request. The Labor and Employee Relations had three months to respond to each question, and they failed. I had already requested extensions to get answers to my questions, and I could not request any more.

I made a request to the Freedom of Information Act for any and all information to include handwritten notes that were gathered, used, or pertained to issuing the Letter of Instructions, issuing and conducting an Internal Affairs Investigation, and issuing a Letter of Reprimand. I made many follow ups via fax, mail, and/or email. The information I was requesting was not classified or sensitive and it was the Freedom of Information Act's responsibility to gather the information and provide it to the requestor. The Freedom of Information Act Office falls under the Executive Director who was in my chain of command, and who I filed many complaints against. I never received the information I requested.

I decided to file an Administrative Grievance to Supervisor 3 for review and action. An Administrative Grievance System is one that the deciding official must be at a higher organizational level than all employees involved in the grievance, and it is reviewed and decided upon within the office I work for, EEO.

CBP Directive for Standard of Conduct speaks about utilizing automated systems that are considered "sensitive but unclassified." "Employees must safeguard all sensitive information against unauthorized disclosure, alteration, or loss. Unauthorized accessing of these systems, including "browsing" (querying the systems for information for other than official reasons) is also prohibited." "Employees will not access, conceal, alter, remove, mutilate, or destroy documents or data in the custody of CBP or the federal government without proper authority".

Complaint System is one that provides the ability to create, track, manage, and report on EEO complaint cases. It contains information for example: name, address, telephone number, work location, Responsible Management Official, and reason why you believe you have been discriminated against.

Supervisor 3 informed me that she received my Administrative Grievance form and supporting documentation. She said the same issue in the Administrative Grievance is in my informal and formal EEO complaints. Supervisor 3 continued to say that it is CBP's policy that duplicative reviews of the same issues(s) in different forums, or under different processes, will not occur. Accordingly, this ends the Administrative Grievance procedure regarding this matter, and there will be no further administrative review.

Supervisor 3 directed me to contact Labor and Employees Relations point of contact for any questions regarding her decision on the Administrative Grievance when she was aware of my attempts to get answers to questions from the Labor and Employee Relations point of contact without a response after many attempts. I did not understand why Supervisor 3 would have me to go back to Labor and Employee Relations point of contact if she could not respond to me before.

I asked Supervisor 3 to answer just one question. My issue filed through the Administrative Grievance process was not an allegation of discrimination; it was based on the Letter of Reprimand for alleged inappropriate use of the Complaint System to create my own complaint and access records on my previous complaints. My EEO complaint was one of discrimination based on reprisal (prior EEO activity) resulting in continuous harassment and a hostile work environment. Based on this information, I asked Supervisor 3 why the Administrative Grievance procedure ended.

Supervisor 3 informed me that I could not pursue the matter through both forums (Administrative Grievance and EEO complaint), and I was not pursuing the same matter (discrimination) in both forums. I informed Supervisor 3 that I reviewed the CBP Directive and the Grievance Decision, and I needed her to help me understand how I could not pursue the matter through both forums.

I requested Supervisor 3 to change her decision, and she said her decision is final. I disagreed with Supervisor 3's decision and Labor and Employee Relations' interpretation of the directive, when it is not stated in the Administrative Grievance, unlike the Negotiated Grievance process, that you cannot file in two venues with the same issue. You would think if it was meant to be according to Labor and Employee Relations, it would be stated in a policy instead of leaving it up to one interpretation that works in favor of management and cannot answer my questions.

I received an email from the manager of the Employee Relations Specialist point of contact and her supervisor. He said that he reviewed my questions, and while each question may not have been answered to my satisfaction, the responses I received were appropriate and accurate. He also mentioned that Supervisor 3 properly found that I was excluded from filing a grievance under CBP's Administrative Grievance System because I initiated the EEO complaint process before filing my grievance.

I requested a thirty-minute in-person meeting with the Executive Director to discuss the Letter of Reprimand, the Letter of Caution, and how I could move forward without further action(s) taken against me when I am not aware, and how I can move forward without looking over my shoulder. I informed my first- and second-line supervisors of my request. The Executive Director declined my visit; therefore, I requested mediation. This mediation was scheduled with Supervisor 3. I was hoping that Supervisor 3 would take into consideration, after hearing from me regarding the matter that lead to the Letter of Reprimand, that she would decide to expunge the Letter of Reprimand from any and all personal, unofficial, and official files.

My allegation was discrimination based on reprisal (prior EEO activity) for filing numerous complaints and a continuous pattern of harassment resulting in a hostile work environment. I also included my civil rights and liberties were violated by not providing my rights.

The Responsible Management Official is the Executive Director for being the Deciding Official to inform Supervisor 3 and having her to inform Supervisor 8 to sign and issue the Letter of Reprimand. The process of receiving this letter started with Supervisor 1 and ended up with Supervisor 8, because she was my supervisor. Only knowledge Supervisor 8 had was one-sided information from management because she did not speak with me prior to issuing the letter to have two-sided information to draw a proper conclusion. The harm I suffered aggravated my pre-existing medical conditions.

During the mediation, I spoke about the Letter of Reprimand, allegations and facts that were stated early on. I said that I did not want to move forward with a complaint. However, I must exercise my right that was presented to me for protection. The Executive Director should not have instructed, informed, or whatever word he used when he was briefed, to give me a Letter of Reprimand for something that I was not aware of until after the fact, and when the action did not continue after I was made aware.

There was no misconduct on my part. There was no violation stated, and CBP policy covers its employees to use CBP information system for official and a limited of personal use. I did not remove or change information in the system. I even informed Supervisor 5 as the Assigning Official. My action was not intentional warranting the rise to the level of a Letter of Reprimand. Speaking about the letter, information included was incorrect and did not fully state the details to show the "real" situation.

I asked Supervisor 3 to expunge any and all personal, unofficial and official files and receive a letter to state it has been done. I had been punished already for this by being counseled by Supervisor 1, by receiving a Letter of Instruction to include denying me access to work on my complaint, by being interrogated by Internal Affairs as if I was a criminal, the wait for some type of action knowing there was no finding, the Executive Director would give me something, and receiving the Letter of Reprimand. Facts do not match conduct and the conduct does not match punishment and I should not be punished on an "assumption that I knew" or "should have known." I ended by saying to Supervisor 3 that all I wanted to do was my job; maintain my health, and enjoy life. The next move is on you. The mediation ended with no resolution just like with the Deputy Director 1 when I attempted to resolve all of my cases with her to move on and she refused.

There was an Internal Affairs investigation regarding this matter; wherein the Executive Director said he had no knowledge and did not know what was happening to me at work. But, he did mention that I should be terminated because I violated the record-keeping policy and that a prior employee was terminated for accessing the EEO records without an official business reason. What the Executive Director failed to say is that in the investigation with this particular employee was found guilty for her actions of looking into other employee records, and I was not.

The Executive Director is totally aware of all aspects of his areas of responsibilities. Remember, he stated that you can go to your congress person, to the Commissioner and to the Secretary of Homeland Security, but it will come back to me.

The Internal Affairs investigation was completed with no findings. They did not charge me with misconduct.

Complaint 11

Denied to Assist Counselor per Procedure

C ounselors are assigned areas of responsibility, and any complaints received that include a request for counseling from those areas will be assigned to that particular counselor. The only time the counselor is not assigned a complaint from their area is if the counselor is on leave, on a special assignment, or sometimes the complainant may ask not to have that particular counselor. This does not always mean that the counselor will be changed. If there is another counselor assigned to a contact outside of their area, that counselor will contact the counselor who would normally handle the complaint in the area to let him or her know they have that particular contact and to ask for general information to assist with counseling. For example: Supervisor 9 contacted me regarding a complaint from his area that I counsel to provide information, to give information, and provide assistance because this is what we had done in the past.

Anyway, I contacted Counselor 4 and said that I had been informed she had a complaint from my area, and she informed me that she could not talk to me about it.

I mentioned that I just wanted to provide information if she needed it. Counselor 4 said that she had someone else on the other line. I asked if she could tell me who told her that she could not speak with me on this case. I cannot remember for sure, but I believe her to say management. I ended the conversation by saying to be careful.

The reason I called Counselor 4 was because I found out that she was typing documents for the complainant to fill in the blanks. Counselor 4 was telling the complainant to file a reprisal against Director, Baltimore Field Operations on a demotion for requesting a desk audit, and the Letter of Reprimand the Director provided to the complainant, in part, to my statement in a meeting when the Director asked me if the complainant contacted me for counseling, and I stated yes, she did. This is when the complainant called me a liar and informed the Counselor that I could not be trusted. I wanted Counselor 4 to be careful in proceeding with this complaint, especially, if what I heard was true. It's what I called "looking after each other." Or was it to catch me off guard in attempts to take action against me?

I wondered if the procedure changed to not assist or provide information on cases in your area to help the counselor? I believe the proper statement should have been something like, "Penny, I am unable to speak with you regarding this case because you have been involved in the case by providing the complainant with information or management. I (Counselor 4) thought it was best due to a conflict of interest not to speak with you." We spoke about trust, working together, and team during the conference, yet I got the "cold shoulder" when I tried to help a counselor.

I contacted Supervisor 3 to see if our procedure changed in assisting another counselor with a case from your area. She wanted to know which complaint I was referring too, how I became aware of it, and who informed me.

I informed Supervisor 3 that I had limited information on this situation. I was leaving a meeting with the Acting Director of Field Operations, and an employee stopped me and asked if I knew Counselor 4, and I said yes. The employee mentioned that she was speaking with Counselor 4 and that is why she was unable to attend the meeting with Director, Baltimore Field Operations and me. I did not question her on the specifics; I just wanted to be clear if it was Counselor 4. When I stated that I was going to give Counselor 4 a call, the employee asked me not to reveal her name. I wanted to contact Counselor 4 to let her know that she is not to complete any forms for the complainant, and if she was doing this to stop and be careful. The counselor's job is to provide the EEO process, gather basic information regarding the complaint and attempt to resolve the complaint. Based on the information and the person (employee), I believe she got the information from the complainant because they worked in the same office. I asked Supervisor 3 if she wanted me to ask the employee if she wanted to reveal her name and provide specific information, and there was no further discussion.

Complaint 12

Special Treatment

I would like to bring up the issue of a coworker disrespecting the Executive Director with her comments three times at our annual EEO conference in front of his staff, which was unprofessional. The reason for bringing this up is to show "special" treatment. What the coworker did was off the chart and well deserving of some type of disciplinary action. Yet, the Executive Director failed to provide disciplinary action to her, but he had no second thoughts of ensuring actions were taken against me. And you wonder why? It was obvious, he liked her, a new employee.

During the conference, he sat in the back of the room beside her, and when it was her time to speak, he slouched down in the chair with his legs stretched out and crossed and his hands together on his stomach, smiling. He slanted his head as she walked to the front of the room with the look of "I want that." I and two other coworkers were in the back rows watching the Executive Director and asking, "Is he really doing this in front of us? Is he going to do anything about the comments she made about how we operate?"

Complaint 13

Denied to Take the Committee Member to EEO Training

One of my responsibilities was the Special Emphasis Program Manager. I had committee members from different locations on the east coast: Boston, New York, Pittsburgh, Baltimore, and Virginia. I spoke with my committee members to see if they wanted to get formal training from the Defense Equal Opportunity Management Institute, Patrick Air Force Base, Florida, and they all said yes. I informed them that they would have to pay for their travel and food, and their rooms would be provided by the institution on base. The only thing left to do was get approval from their supervisors for either administrative leave for training or use their annual leave. The committee members said if they had to use their leave, they would use it for a chance to go to Florida for formal training. The committee members received approval from their supervisors, so I contacted the training personnel at the Defense Equal Opportunity Management Institute and set everything up for the next training, which was a few months away. We were ready to go, at least I thought we were.

I informed my supervisor, Supervisor 8, and requested approval to use administrative leave, and I was denied. I requested to use my annual leave, and since management cannot deny me to use my annual leave, they said that I could not take the committee members to this training when there was training in our office. Supervisor 8 said if the committee members need training then I could give it to them at my location in person or by a conference call. I informed the committee members that I could not go, they could go without me, but they did not want to. There were no official reasons to deny me permission to take my committee members to this training and have them miss this opportunity— except for personal reasons.

Received a Letter of Caution

Supervisor 8 issued me a Letter of Caution for discouraging an employee from filing an EEO complaint and failing to perform my duties "respectively". She said that this was not a disciplinary action, but just to caution me on how my actions may appear to others, and remind me since I had an active reprimand on file, any misconduct that is substantiated may result in further disciplinary action.

Supervisor 8 said that she expected me to adhere to the laws concerning pre-complaint processing and individual complaints as defined by the Code of Federal Regulations and EEO MD-110. She also encouraged me to review the materials I received from the Sailing through the Federal Sector EEO Process course, which discussed the processes for handling EEO complaints.

She told me that this letter was not a disciplinary action; therefore, it would not be a matter of record in my Official Personnel Folder; nonetheless, she strongly urged me to pay close attention to its content and intent.

I informed Supervisor 8 that I could not understand why I received the Letter of Caution if the case was closed. I provided an example of a coworker, a similar situated employee outside of my protected group who was treated more favorably. Supervisor 8 wanted me to hurry up and read the letter, sign it, and send it back to her. I expressed my thoughts that I would review the letter very carefully and pray on what happened and my response to her.

In my response I said that I would like to thank Supervisor 8 for giving me the opportunity to ask questions unlike the Letter of Reprimand. I shared with her that I informed God that I forgave her, Supervisor 1, Supervisor 2, and the Executive Director for what they had knowingly done to me, and I asked Him to give me strength to get through the "bogus" actions to either force me to resign or retire or terminate me for prior EEO activity. I also wrote that I believed the Letter of Caution was a form of reprisal for prior EEO activity and represented the continuous harassment against me that had resulted in a hostile and violent work place. I said Supervisor 8, Supervisor 1, Supervisor 3, and the Executive Director had physically and mentally ruined my career and health through selfish actions against me over the years with cover ups.

I would like to show what was in the Letter of Caution, the comments and questions I asked Supervisor 8, and Supervisor 8's response to my questions.

1. The Letter of Caution included two allegations: discouraged an employee from filing an EEO complaint and failure to perform duties. Instead of having a spin-off complaint for dissatisfaction of the process as we have done in the past, there was an Internal Affairs investigation, and that investigation included one allegation of the complainant. Supervisor 8 charged me with

another offense, when I was not informed, and it was not part of the investigation per the investigator when he contacted me. I asked Supervisor 8 the reason why he contacted me? I asked what was the purpose of this allegation? Supervisor 8's response was that both complainants made allegations that I violated an EEO regulation in the form of dissuading them from filing a complaint.

2. The Letter of Caution stated Supervisor 8 expected me to adhere to the laws concerning pre-complaint processing. Since Supervisor 8 had been my supervisor, this was the first incident that I was aware of. She mentioned another case in a telephone conversation that involved a gay poster. As I recall, Supervisor 8 was aware through my briefings with her that the complainant's immediate complaint was to resolve with management removing the poster. The other part of the complaint was the complainant wanted to file a complaint about the proclamation of having Lesbian, Gay, Bisexual, and Transgender Pride Month I informed the complainant of his options so he could decide what to do; this case was never brought up as an issue, so I asked "Why now?" Supervisor 8's response was that the answer was in the complainant's case; he also alleged that I dissuaded him from filing a complaint.

3. The Letter of Caution stated that "this letter serves to caution you to be cognizant of how

your actions may appear to others..." I asked Supervisor 8 to please explain because I cannot control what others may think, say, or do. I can only control me and performing my duties in a professional matter, which I have. Supervisor 8's response was that she believed the statement was self-explanatory.

4. I requested the status of the Internal Affairs investigation, and Supervisor 8 told me that she would be fair with the decision. Was it "fair" to add another allegation without notifying me and giving me the opportunity to respond? Why wasn't this allegation added to the Internal Affairs investigation? Supervisor 8's response was that two complainants alleged that I dissuaded them from filing complaints. Both were included in the Report of Investigation.

5. I asked Supervisor 8 what I needed *not* to do in counseling to prevent any actions against me. Supervisor 8 said that I was an EEO Specialist, and as such, she should not have to tell me how to counsel. I did not ask her to tell me how to counsel. I asked her to tell me what I was doing incorrectly. If I was being charged with action for one person out of so many overall how could I prevent this from occurring in the future? I asked Supervisor 8 to provide specific information that would assist me in counseling to prevent this incident or one like it from reoccurring. Supervisor 8's response was that we

could have a discussion concerning this. The discussion never happened.

6. I had with one person complain, out of many contacts and informal complaints, that ended in an Internal Affairs investigation. This being the case, how can you tell me to adhere to the laws concerning Pre-complaint Processing and Individual Complaints and review the materials from the Sailing through the Federal Sector EEO process course? Supervisor 8's response was that the statement is self-explanatory given the allegations that were raised.

7. What is it that you, Supervisor 1, and the Executive Director want of me, so I can move forward in performing my duties without looking over my shoulder? Supervisor 8's response was that she expected me to adhere to the laws concerning Pre-complaint Processing and Individual Complaints as defined by the Code of Federal Regulations and Equal Employment Opportunity MD-110.

8. Can this Letter of Caution be rescinded? If not, I would like to exercise my right in utilizing my chain of command to speak with Supervisor 3. Supervisor 8 responded that she would not rescind the Letter of Caution. Supervisor 3 said that she would not rescind the Letter of Caution. I asked to speak with the Executive Director, and he refused to speak with me.

Let me tell you about Supervisor 8. I remember when I came on board, she was a coworker under the same supervisor. She used to ask me questions about the complaint process based on my experience and we used to have a lot of conversations on the telephone laughing, joking, and just talking about the office. All was fine until the day she became my Counselor when I filed a complaint. She told me that Supervisor 3 had her erase information on the computer regarding my complaint. Because of my relationship with the Counselor, she informed me. I told the Counselor that I would not tell anyone. My case was investigated; I was asked a lot of questions, but I did not tell the investigator what the Counselor told me not to say. The investigator spoke with the Counselor. She thought I told the investigator what she told me, and she turned the story around to blame me. I did not know this until I received the Report of Investigation. From that point, I stopped speaking with the Counselor because I did not trust her. About three years later, she became my Supervisor 8. Working with her was not healthy or professional. She tried her best to get me terminated coming up with trumped-up charges or situations and having management to back her up or say that she told me something when she did not. This was payback.

Supervisor 8 had no reason to be a supervisor because she did not know how to supervise. Supervisor 8 did not have good written and speaking communication, conflict resolution, leadership, critical thinking, interpersonal skills, problem solving, building relations, motivating her employees, and I can go on. Just look at her responses to me.

But when you suck up to management, qualifications are thrown out the window, so they can get what they want.

Complaint 15

Denied Veterans Affairs Non-Paid Work Experience Duties

Another part of my responsibility was the Outreach Program. I looked into the Veterans Affairs Non-Paid Work Experience Program to bring it to the Baltimore Field Office where I was located. I received approval from Supervisor 9 to work on this project, but Supervisor 1 wanted to be kept abreast. I sent Supervisor 1 an email on my visit to the Department of Veterans Affairs, Vocational Rehabilitation and Employment Division, Baltimore Regional Office with the Employment Coordinator about partnership with the Baltimore Field Office to introduce their Non-Paid Work Experience Program for Veterans.

This program was similar to the Wounded Warrior Program with the following exceptions: the recipients had to be a veteran, disabled, and out of the military searching employment. The good thing about this program was that it was free to CBP. The Vocational Rehabilitation and Employment Division would pay for the veteran training. The Employment Coordinator had a veteran ready to go.

I provided Supervisor 1 a briefing packet with slides for further information. I informed her that this was a great program for us to work with Vocational Rehabilitation to help veterans, and I asked her to let me know what she thought.

Supervisor 1 briefed the Executive Director, Deputy Director 1, and Assistant Director for Diversity and Compliance. They all agreed it was an excellent program and they were referring the program to Human Resources Management for their Veterans Recruitment Program to take over.

Supervisor 1 knew I was working on this program and at no time did she tell me that the EEO Office transitioned all of its veteran programs to Human Resources Management. I did the work for the Baltimore Field Office and the project was removed from me. Supervisor 1 informed me that this project was a wonderful initiative that I had uncovered and cultivated, and I would receive credit for the "great find!" I received no credit recognition, award letter or nothing.

Complaint 16

Years Delay with Service Award

I have sat in conference calls where the Executive Director would acknowledge employees for the number of years of service and provide them with service awards. I started thinking that I had not received one. I should have received one at my tenth year and then my fifteenth year. I recall at one of the conference calls that an employee said that she had not received her service award. I contacted Supervisor 9 via email about my award and complained.

During another conference call, the Executive Director was acknowledging employees for their years in service. He sounded excited with a high pitch as he called the names out and even said nice words to them. Another name was called, but the pitch was low and the tone of voice indicated a lack of interest, unlike the others. Afterward, I called one of my coworkers to ask about the person whose name I could not hear because there was no excitement in the voice saying the name and the years of service. The coworker said it was me. The Executive Director could not get excited about my time with the federal government but had no problem expressing happiness and excitement for the other employees who were receiving awards.

Complaint 17

Denied Training

Supervisor 9 informed me that I was required to submit an Individual Development Plan. When I submitted the form with the training that I wish to take to improve my job at a very low cost, I was denied.

Supervisor 9 said there is no money available for training. For me to identify development training at no cost. Virtual Learning Center, Department of Veteran Affairs, and maybe the military base could provide me training at no cost.

I informed Supervisor 9 that the EEO Headquarters asked if anyone was interested in attending the Administrative Inquiry Training and I said I was. The EEO Headquarters sent someone else without notifying me. I requested to go to the Defense Equal Opportunity Management Institute for training which there was no cost to the EEO Office, and I was denied. I requested to go to a free conference in Baltimore even Supervisor 6 backed me up because I was here in Baltimore. Instead the EEO Office paid for a staff member from Headquarters, Washington, DC, to come to Baltimore. I asked for a detail at no cost for development and I was denied, and there were other free training requests I made and I was denied.

I informed Supervisor 9 that the Virtual Learning Center, a computer-type training could not develop me. The Executive Director's, Supervisor 1's, and Supervisor 3's actions along with the actions they allowed to take place against me by supervisors and employees over the years was forcing me to retire. I continued looking over my shoulder for the next action they would take against me. Managers and supervisors had ruined my health and career, and they enjoyed doing it. I also told Supervisor 9 that my individual development was surviving until I could retire, and that he would not understand why I felt that way unless he had walked in my shoes.

Complaint 18

Denied Work Station Accommodation

S upervisor 9 submitted a request for a Workstation Evaluation regarding a potential problem with my workstation. I had an evaluation and was informed that I needed a gel wrist pad for my keyboard to eliminate strain to my wrists, a foot stool/rest to accommodate the height of my chair, and a document holder. This evaluation was sent to Supervisor 9. I followed up with Supervisor 9 a few times but never received the wrist pad and foot stool; I received only a document holder that I could not use. I believe Supervisor 9 did what he could to try to get the equipment I needed for my work station, but he had to go through his supervisor, Supervisor 1, for approval of the funds. I never received the gel wrist pad and the foot stool/rest.

Considering a New Assignment

D uring one of my visits with my daughter in California, there was an assignment opening for an EEO Specialist in Long Beach, California. I asked Supervisor 3 if I could be responsible for that area and move to California. Supervisor 3 said sure. On my way home to Maryland, I started thinking that if I moved to California and started to work in a new area under a new supervisor with the formal stage of the Complaint Processing (an area that I had worked for many years with another agency), the Executive Director would get his way by removing me. Think about it: new environment, new assignment, and new Supervisor 4 who had already proven she would do as the Executive Director told her, even when his instructions were against policy. He would have her show that I could not perform the job.

You remember, the Executive Director instructed Supervisor 4 to open my closed Report of Investigation that an EEOC Hearing was requested to add false information to discredit me. Wherein, the information should have been sent to the EEOC Hearing for them to make the decision to add the information or not. Most importantly, the Executive Director should have waited for the Internal Affairs investigation to be completed for the decision. Had he waited, the information would not have been submitted to the EEOC. The decision was on the table to take the new assignment or keep my assignment. I decided to stay with what I knew and kept my current assignment because I knew how this office wanted things done and it would be harder for the Executive Director to terminate me.

Comment During Mediation

I was scheduled to have a conference call with the Executive Director, EEOC Administrative Judge, and the Executive Director's two CBP counsels to attempt resolution through mediation. The Executive Director refused or declined being on the conference call with me. During the call, I mentioned that I was retiring in two years. The judge asked me how old I was because I sounded young. I had no problem telling the judge my age. He informed counsels to "let me retire in peace." Needless to say, that did not happen. I was always looking over my shoulder for the next situation. Some of my work was taken away, and Supervisor 9 and I would get into quite a few disagreements that kept going on and on.

In all of my requests for help to stop management's behavior, the administrative judge was the first person who stood up for me even though the behavior did not stop.

Complaint 21

Disputed Request for Leave

I submitted three requests for sick leave for three different dates in different months to Supervisor 9 due to the harassment, a hostile work environment, mistreatment, and its aftereffects while employed. Supervisor 9 wanted to have a meeting regarding my requests. I told him that I did not understand the purpose of the meeting to discuss the leave I submitted. I mentioned that he was aware of some of the things that took place, my constant battle looking back, how I was treated, and that I continually looked over my shoulder for the next action. I informed him that I hoped he approved my leave because had it not been for what supervisors and managers had done to me, I could save my leave and money.

Supervisor 9 said that he has been my supervisor for the last year and few months, and that he had "not harassed me in any way, shape, or form." I told Supervisor 9 that we had gone over this in the past. This was not about him, but working under him for a year and maybe two months did not take away what had happened to me in seven years. I told Supervisor 9 that if he did not understand or didn't want to understand, there was nothing I could do about that. I just did not want to continue the conversation and to know that this was not about him. I had filed a number of complaints based on harassment and hostile work environment and was seeking help to overcome what had happened to me, and I told him that I still looked over my shoulder for the next action until my forced retirement comes. I told Supervisor 9 that he was aware of this. My request was for sick leave not for Office of Worker's Compensation or to file an informal EEO complaint.

Supervisor 9 could not let this go. He said that he was not forcing me to retire nor was he personally aware of the alleged harassments incidents. I told Supervisor 9 that I did not understand why he was taking this personally. I did not say he was forcing me to retire. The treatment that I had received from management and some supervisors while working for the EEO that affected my health and career is forcing me to retire. I said he is aware of some situations that have occurred because I told him.

Supervisor 9 said that I had mentioned some of the situations that may have occurred. He was just indicating that he had no direct knowledge (personally aware) of them. He said as my supervisor, he wanted to make sure I know that he in no way was forcing me to retire. Supervisor 9 said that I brought lots of experience to the job and often helped him think outside of the box, and this, in his opinion, was good collaboration.

I asked Supervisor 9 why he continued going back and forward on this matter. Based on my experience working with him as my supervisor, I would not file a complaint against him, and he was not forcing me to retire. The damage had already been done to me. I had to deal with this damage until I met the requirements to retire.

I knew that Supervisor 9 wanted to stay out of this. When situations came up as I was speaking with him, I would mention what happened to me. I did share that he could not imagine what I had gone through. The issue escalated to the point of the Executive Director calling me because I went to his supervisor regarding his behavior of threatening and intimidating me and my career to have an anxiety attack that sent me to the hospital. Then he, the Executive Director, said that I did not have a work-related injury, that he only called me about my harassment complaint; it was about him. I told Supervisor 9 either he did not understand or he did not want to understand. I asked that we not continue this conversation because it was taking me back.

Received Written Counseling Statement Based on a Complainant's Complaint

Supervisor 9 sent an email to me following up on our discussion of a complainant's email alleging that I provided my personal opinion during my conversation with her, which she found insulting, and she believed she was given false information about overtime assignments while on light duty.

Let me mention this first: Supervisor 9 and I had a telephone conversation where he asked me information about my telephone call with this complainant. I provided the information he requested, and then he sent me an email regarding the same matter. You know this was done to have written documentation against me for action.

Supervisor 9 mentioned that I already knew EEO counselors were to assist potential complainants in defining their complaints and are required to try to informally resolve their complaints. Based on the complainant's email and my reply, Supervisor 9 said it was not clear whether or not I provided my personal opinion, however, I may have provided erroneous information concerning Overtime Assignments During Light Duty. Therefore, he provided me with CBP policy to attempt resolution of discrimination complaints at the earliest possible point in the administrative process. He also provided the primary role in counseling, information contained in the union contract, CBP's Light Duty Policy concerning overtime work and assignment, and the CBP Directive on Temporary Light Duty to serve as reminders.

Now, providing me with information about my job when I knew it and had been doing it longer than Supervisor 9 was insulting.

I responded to Supervisor 9 that if I recalled correctly, he wanted to speak with me about an email he received from a complainant. I asked about it, and time went on. Finally, we had a brief conversation. He expressed that he wanted to send me an email, and I mentioned that I did not want it because he would be like the other managers who sent me emails then waited for my response so they could then issue me a written counseling statement.

I gathered from our conversation that there would not be any counseling regarding this matter. Yet, he sent me a (politically correct) written counseling statement about my responsibilities because I *might* have provided incorrect information not because I provided incorrect information. If not, our verbal conversation should have put this matter to rest.

I told Supervisor 9 that I provided the complainant information on the EEO process, and since she was a union member, I had a copy of the National Collective Bargaining Agreement that I read to her; I read the article pertaining to her questions. I also gave her the article number, title, and page numbers. There was no incorrect information that I provided, and I did not insult her. Since she was pregnant, I did ask her to take care of herself and be careful at the end of our conversation because she was upset when she contacted me. I guess she contacted my supervisor because she did not hear what she wanted to hear.

I informed Supervisor 9 of the harassment, hostile environment, threats, intimidation, and the attempts to terminate me in the years I worked for the Executive Director, Supervisor 1, Supervisor 3, Supervisor 8, and a few other supervisors. I wanted to help the complainants by providing them as much information as possible so they could make an intelligent decision in the attempt to resolve their concerns or complaints, and this had always been my payback.

Supervisor 9 informed me that this was not disciplinary in nature, all he wanted to do was memorialize what was discussed so there was no confusion down the line. I informed him that he could call it whatever he wanted. I had been there; therefore, this is a written counseling statement. If not, as I stated, our conversation would have put this matter to rest. How many other employees when someone filed a complaint against them received this type of letter and/or an Internal Affairs investigation? The purpose of speaking to each other is to get an understanding what happened, when you result to writing the same thing you spoke about, it is a form of action taken. I informed Supervisor 9 that I had no further comment about this matter.

Complaint 23

Instructed to Add Name in Complaint System When Complainant Requested to Be Anonymous

A complainant contacted me and stated that she wanted to be anonymous, and that she did not want her information to be placed in our Complaints System; therefore, I did not ask for her personal information, and she did not tell me. She just needed someone to talk to. Because our Standard Operating Procedure was to input all contacts in the Complaint System, I inputted the telephone call, but not the complainant's personal information.

Supervisor 9 saw that I inputted anonymous at the name and questioned me. He informed me that I needed to input the individual personal contact information in the system. We went back and forth, and I kept saying that the complainant asked to be anonymous. She did not want her information in our Complaints System. Needless to say, based on my conversation with Supervisor 9, I had to call the complainant back and tell her that although she asked to be anonymous, I had to get her information to input in the system. I informed the complainant that it was my understanding that no one would contact her, that it is just for stats only. I received the information and input it into the system.

I sent an email to Supervisor 9 letting him know that I disagreed with providing the name of my complainant. However, because of past action taken against me and fear of present action taken if I did not reveal the complainant's name, I listed it in the Complaint System per his request. I further said that if anything comes out of this because of the EEO Office action forcing me to release the name will be the EEO Office's responsibility.

Confidentiality is an ethical concern. It is to protect a complainant's right to privacy when requested by ensuring matters disclosed not be relayed to others without the informed consent of the complainant. The complainant requested not to have her name revealed and the EEO Office forced me to reveal her name.

Complaint 24

Denied Knowing of the Hostile Work Environment

I sent Supervisor 9 an email after he asked me "who in management was creating a hostile work environment and what specifically are they doing?" I responded to Supervisor 9 asking him not to play on my intelligence as if he was not aware. I was asked the reason why I was retiring, and I stated the reasons. I said Supervisor 9 is aware of my reasons because I told him. My chain of command is aware of the harassment and hostile work environment because I told them. Therefore, I said if he wanted to know the details of the harassment and hostile work environment again, I suggest he get a copy of my book when it comes out. The reason for leaving my job is being forced to retire due to management's treatment against me, injuries sustained, and a hostile work environment. I informed Supervisor 9 that I did not wish to entertain this subject again with him due to my health.

Complaint 25

Denied Award

When Supervisor 2 was my supervisor, she submitted two requests for an award to Supervisor 1 for me and Supervisor 1 denied them both. However, other EEO specialists that had done less, received awards. In addition, Supervisor 7 denied me an end-of-the-year award. I have never received an award in all the years I worked for the EEO Office, not even for my outreach activity with Morgan State University, which you will read under Complaint 26 or the development of the Veterans Program for the Baltimore Field Office.

Complaint 26

Denied Acknowledgement of Accomplishment

E very week, Deputy Director 2 would send out an email regarding different subjects. One in particular I received waiting to see if he would mention me in talking about outreach activities, which he did not, so I sent him an email saying:

This is in response to your email. You said, "Thanks to all who take the time to respond to these messages. It's always good hearing from you, and your feedback is greatly appreciated. Your hard work gets noticed!"

I introduced myself and said I was physically located at the Baltimore Field Office, Baltimore, Maryland, which was less than fifty miles from him. I had never spoken with him over the telephone or in person. However, I had been watching his emails to see if he would say anything about me as far as outreach activities like I have seen in the past. For example: EEO specialists, El Paso, Texas, he commented on being a great job because the EEO specialists spoke with a university regarding outreach activities. If this is "hard work" that "gets noticed," what happened to what I had done for about the past seven years. Let me say, I wrote, that since he had been putting out these emails, nothing. I informed him about my "hard work" with Morgan State University and the Baltimore Field Office, Director, Baltimore Field Operations, because this was on his watch.

I said that I had guest speakers from the Baltimore Field Office, Headquarters and Counsel speak at Morgan State University on organizational leadership and ethics, integrity, human resource management, managing employees' performance, separating and retaining employees, analyzing work, and designing jobs, planning and recruiting, selecting employees and placing them in jobs, training employees, establishing a pay structure, recognizing employee contributions with pay, providing employee benefits, and much more.

After each speaking engagement, Morgan State University provided a thank-you letter. Here are some of the comments from the students: "Excellent...," "Inspiring...," "Mind-blowing...," "I wasn't expecting this...," "So energizing...," "It gave me hope..." "Speakers helped me understand and feel the responsibility of being a leader, including the need to be attentive to each and every follower."

My note continued that I could go on and on. I always attached these letters to the Complaint System, and was no secret that my chain of command, all the way up to the Executive Director, was aware of these activities. Based on my experience, I could understand why Deputy Director 2 had never mentioned me. I shared that I brought this up to him because of his statement, "Your hard work gets noticed!" And my hard work building and maintaining a relationship with Morgan State University for about seven years by sending guest speakers who touched each student in a profound way got no notice.

I informed the Deputy Director 2 that there was no need to respond to my email. I just wanted him to know there was an employee whose "hard work" was never noticed by this organization. I said, just in case he was wondering why didn't I say something sooner, it was because I had ten working days left, so the managers could not take action against me for speaking out anymore.

Complaint 27

Force to Retire

I sent the Federal Retirement Benefits an email informing them that everything in the Federal Retirement Benefits was correct except for the type of retirement. Mine was a forced retirement, not a voluntary retirement.

I submitted a request to the Retirement and Benefits Advisory Services. I included a subject line that read: Involuntary Retirement in-lieu of Voluntary Retirement. In my request I said, "This packet serves to provide limited information on why involuntary retirement in-lieu of voluntary retirement must be approved." Since I did not know the required information to provide for involuntary retirement, I sent twenty attachments that explained how being subjected to harassment and hostile work environment by the Executive Director and his managers and supervisors resulted in physical and mental injuries. In particular, when the Executive Director contacted me via telephone, using his position and authority to intentionally threaten, harass, and intimidate me, which placed me in a dangerous position, and I fainted and sustained a head injury because I sought help by going to his supervisor, the Commissioner, because of his and his managers' behavior toward me.

My involuntary retirement was based on endangering my health and welfare during my employment with CBP, EEO Office. Had it not been for this abuse, I would still be working. I met the requirements of age and service, minimum civilian service, separation from a position subject to Civilian Service Retirement Act coverage, and disability or illness or endangering one's health. If there was a doubt, an advance advisory opinion from the Office of Personnel could be requested, which I made that request. I was unable to get a response unless I stayed past the requested retirement date to get a decision or unless my chain of command provided a statement that I was being terminated.

If I stayed past my retirement date, my work environment would not have changed, and my health would have been at risk. I had no idea how long this process would take. I felt that I provided enough documentation that the EEO Office endangered my health and the decision should have been made. My medical provider wanted me to retire at the very first date that I could retire due to my health, so I retired. Per clearing from the EEO Office, I inputted "forced retirement" on my clearance form because if my work environment was about business and being professional and not personal, I still would be working.

Complaint 28

Failure to Present Retirement Letter

The Baltimore Field Office wanted to have a retirement party for me to show their appreciation for the nine years that I served them. They requested the EEO Office to provide a letter to me for the years I worked for them. This is standard operating procedure when a person retired to provide them with an award letter and/or money. However, the Executive Director did not want to provide anything. The Director of the Baltimore Field Operations contacted the EEO Office Executive Director and stated he should do the right thing and provide a letter. The day of the event, Deputy Director 2 brought the letter to the Baltimore Field Office but failed to attend the event to represent the office I work for and to provide the letter to me. Instead, the Baltimore Field Office representative read the letter and provided it to me.

Do you see how much hatred the Executive Director had against me? He did not want to give me a letter and then he refused having someone from the office I worked to present it to me. This behavior should not have been tolerated in the workplace.

RECOMMENDATIONS

Recommendations for Improving the EEO Program

You have to ask the question: Do we all have equal employment opportunities in the work place? If the answer is no then we need to take actions and make some changes for all employees. I would suggest first to change the EEO name.

Have a name that stands for all human beings or people without putting them in categories, as on the basis of race, color, religion, sex, national origin, disability, genetic information, or reprisal. People mistreated in the workplace does not always fall into one of the bases. All employees that are being mistreated in the workplace should be able to file a complaint to one office instead of many depending on the situation, for example: EEO, Administrative Grievance, Internal Affairs, Inspector General… Multiple necessary filings can be confusing to an employee seeking help and can deter an employee from seeking help. Therefore, the name should represent an office that deals with all complaints of mistreatment in the workplace that is outside of the agency the employee works for, so supervisors and managers cannot interfere, and so those responsible can be held accountable for their actions against the employee.

Change the Equal Employment Opportunity Program

As long as the EEO Complaint Program is within the agency the employee works for, management will control the process and the employee will not receive fair treatment. Therefore, I recommend the changes, which are not limited to the following:

1. Remove the Equal Employment Opportunity Complaint (Informal/Formal) Processes from all agencies.
2. Place the program under one agency with a new name for the agency and a new title for the employees.
3. Any employees working the informal and formal processes will have to work for the one agency with the new name at their location.
4. The employee chain of command will be the new agency with the new name.
5. Any mistreatment in the workplace should be resolved first by the chain of command prior to filing a complaint to the new agency with the new name that includes written documentation of the attempts.
6. Have all complaints from all agencies go to the new agency with the new name for processing.

7. The new agency with the new name will set up the employees to process each complaint with no interference from the agencies the complaints come from.

8. Change the timeframe for processing all complaints to include class-action complaints to a lesser timeframe.

9. Managers and supervisors involved in a complaint will have to obtain their own attorney, the same as employees.

10. Based on the information provided, the new agency with the new name will make the decision whether the employee was mistreated or not with no involvement from the agency.

11. This process will be one like the court system. A complainant filed a claim against the supervisor and/or manager and the administrative judge makes the decision based on facts.

12. Any money judgement is forwarded to the financial institution for collection. The agency will no longer pay for managers and/or supervisors' actions against employees.

13. Judgements other than "money" will go to the manager or supervisor chain of command to take action on the judgement per written documentation.

14. Managers and/or supervisors will have the right to appeal.

15. Streamlining the process will decrease the cost for each complaint filed (instead of paying between $25,000 and $300,000), save time, result in less complaints filed and actions taken against employees, encourage all to move forward to mission accomplishment.

Change the Special Emphasis Program

I sent the former President of the United States an email, the subject I provided was: EEO Program (Diversity and Cutting Cost for Complaints). I reminded the former President of his statement that he wanted to bring the country together. I said one way he could accomplish this was through the Equal Employment Opportunity Program. Currently we are continuing to separate people instead of bringing them together through the Special Emphasis Program by having separate observances for some but not all groups, to include white males. I informed the former President that I believed this was a time for "change." It was time to have one program during the year that would address all cultural groups and would go back to the basics and educate all groups through in-person training like in the '60s or '70s, not how training is conducted today via the internet. In doing so, we would save money and time, and would bring people together through understanding and create change.

I informed the former President that if he considers having the EEOC regulation changed, I would like to be on the committee. I received no response.

Stop Managers' and Supervisors' Actions against Employees

If an employee applies for a position and gets that position, that employee should be able to perform the duties as trained within the timeframe agreed upon without any wrong treatment. If that employee suffers mistreatment from the supervisor or manager then:

1. Managers and/or supervisors must be held accountable for their actions against an employee.
2. Their chain of command must be held accountable for taking appropriate action against a manager and/or supervisor for their unfavorable treatment against an employee.
3. The manager and/or supervisor's chain of command must hold the manager and/or supervisor to the policies and procedures of the organization as relate to fairness and respectful treatment of the employees.
4. The chain of command of the manager and/or supervisor must have their hands on the "pause of the organization" (status of work production, number of complaints, number of employees leaving, many changes, and talking with the employees) and take appropriate action when needed.

5. Managers and/or supervisors' chain of command must be actively involved to ensure proper work production and a safe and healthy work environment for the employees.

6. If managers and/or supervisors go against policy and procedures in subjecting employees to an unsafe and unhealthy work environment, then their chain of command should provide them with a verbal counseling, written counseling, Letter of Reprimand, and up to termination with their official record being noted depending on the number of times a manager and/or supervisor has gone against the policy and procedures to show this type of behavior will not be tolerated.

7. Managers and/or supervisors should not be given a slap on the hand because of who they are or who they know, and they should not be moved to another location to cause issues there.

8. Managers and/or supervisors will not have access to the agency attorney, the same as employees. If they need an attorney, they will have to pay for their own, just like employees.

9. Managers and/or supervisors will not have access to no other source of the agency to help their case or situation just like the employees. For example: Labor and Employee Relations, Human Resources, Counsel...

10. Any settlement of payment will be the responsibility of managers and/or supervisors not the agency.

11. Taking this action will not only cease and desist managers and/or supervisor's inappropriate actions against employees, but it will save the government funds.

NOTE PAGE

This NCO Knows about Discrimination

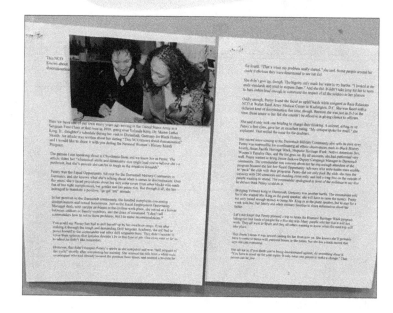

Job Titles

The constant changes to office personnel and duties is the reason you see so many of the same positions stated below. The people that held these positions were involved in actions taken against me.

1. Executive Director
2. Deputy Director 1
3. Deputy Director 2
4. Supervisor 1 (Director)
5. Supervisor 2 (Director)
6. Supervisor 3 (Director)
7. Supervisor 4 (Director)
8. Supervisor 5 (Assistant Director/Coworker)
9. Supervisor 6 (Assistant Director/Coworker)
10. Supervisor 7(Assistant Director)
11. Supervisor 8 (Assistant Director/Coworker)
12. Supervisor 9 (Assistant Director/Team Leader/Coworker)
13. Acting Supervisor (Coworker)
14. Assistant Director 1 (Coworker)
15. Assistant Director 2 (Coworker)
16. Counselor 1 (Coworker)
17. Counselor 2 (Coworker)
18. Counselor 3 (Coworker)
19. Counselor 4 (Coworker)

Abbreviations

Department of Homeland Security	**DHS**
Customs and Border Protection	**CBP**
Equal Employment Opportunity Commission	**EEOC**
Internal Affairs	**IA**
Joint Intake Center	**JIC**
Inspector General	**IG**
Office of Special Counsel	**OSC**
Labor and Employee Relations	**LER**
Employee Relations	**ER**
Office of Personnel Management	**OPM**
Office of Diversity and Civil Rights	**ODCR**
Equal Employment Opportunity Office	**EEOO**

Human Resources Office	**HRO**
Director of Field Operations	**DFO**
Director of Baltimore Field Operations	**DBFO**
Diversity and Inclusion	**DIC**
Retirement and Benefit Advising Services	**RABAS**
Federal Employed Retirement System	**FERS**
Workers Compensation Office	**WCO**
Freedom of Information Act	**FOIA**
Report of Investigation	**ROI**
Notice of Right to File	**NORTF**
Executive Office	**EO**
Assistant Director	**AD**
Micropact Internet Complaints System	**MICS**

EEO Complaint Process

Informal Stage

1. You must initiate contact with an EEO Counselor within 45 days of the date of the alleged discriminatory act or within 45 days of the effective date of the personnel or employment action. This action begins the informal process for initiating the discrimination complaint.

2. You will have a choice of participating either in EEO counseling or in mediation. If you choose counseling, the Counselor has within 30 days to counsel your complaint and issue the Notice of Right to File. If you choose mediation, the counselor has within 90 days to mediate your complaint where there may be a settlement or no settlement. If you decide mediation, it is conducted at the discretion of the agency.

3. If you do not settle the complaint during mediation, you can file a formal discrimination complaint within 15 days from the day you receive the Notice of Right to File a Discrimination Complaint.

Formal Stage

1. Once you filed a formal complaint, the agency will review the complaint and decide whether or not the case should be accepted, dismissed, amended or consolidated.
2. If the complaint is accepted, the agency has within 180 days to investigate and provide a Report of Investigation.
3. During this timeframe, you have an option of mediation to settle the case or no mediation. If you decide mediation, it is conducted at the discretion of the agency. If you decide not to settle, you can request a hearing before an EEOC Administrative Judge or ask the agency to issue a final agency decision as to whether the discrimination occurred within 30 days.
4. If you ask the agency to issue a final decision and no discrimination is found, or you disagree with some part of the final decision, you can appeal the decision to EEOC or challenge it in the federal district court.

Hearing Stage

1. If you request a hearing, an EEOC Administrative Judge will conduct the hearing, decide, and order relief if discrimination is found within 180 days.
2. Once the agency receives the Administrative Judge's decision, the agency will issue a final order which will tell you whether the agency agrees with the Administrative Judge and if it

will grant any relief in the ordered. The agency will have 40 days to issue the final order.

3. You have the right to appeal an agency's final order to the EEOC Office of Federal Operations no later than 30 days after you receive the final order.

4. If you disagree with the EEOC's decision on your appeal, you can request a reconsideration of that decision. This request is only granted if you can show that the decision is based on a mistake about the facts of the case or the law applied to the facts. You must request for a reconsideration no later than 30 days after you receive the decision on the appeal.

5. Once the decision is made on the reconsideration, it is final.

6. Complainant can file a civil action within 90 days of the Final Agency Decision or EEOC's Final Decision.

Regulations, Policies and Standard Operating Procedures

Title VII of the Civil Rights Act of 1964 (Title VII)

"This law makes it illegal to discriminate against someone on the basis of race, color, religion, national origin, or sex. The law also makes it illegal to retaliate against a person because the person complained about discrimination, filed a charge of discrimination, or participated in an employment discrimination investigation or lawsuit".

Privacy and Diversity EEO Policy

Commissioner's Message: Workplace Free from Harassment and Discrimination

"At U.S. Customs and Border Protection, we are committed to transparency and accountability in accomplishing our mission. We must bring that same dedication to ensuring each employee understands and complies with CBP's anti-discrimination and anti-harassment policies. The official policy statement is detailed and specific – read the statement to learn your obligations under CBP's Standards of Conduct. It affirms our commitment to equal opportunity and to the fair treatment of all CBP employees, applicants for employment, and members of the trade and traveling public. The policy also prohibits discriminatory harassment. CBP policy requires all employees to report misconduct, which includes discriminatory or harassing behavior. We will address reports with a thorough and impartial investigation; where allegations are substantiated, appropriate action will be taken. All CBP employees have the right to work in an environment free from discrimination and harassment. Every CBP employee is responsible for ensuring this happens. Join me in fostering an environment of equality, fairness and respectful treatment of our coworkers, job applicants and the public we serve. Pledging to uphold these values helps us succeed in maintaining integrity, vigilance and service to our country."

Commissioner

Anti-Discrimination and Anti-Harassment Policy Statement

"As the Deputy Commissioner of U.S. Customs and Border Protection (CBP), Performing the Duties of the Commissioner of CBP, I want to affirm that unlawful discrimination, the unfavorable treatment of a person or class of persons based on their protected status under Federal law, is strictly prohibited. It is CBP's policy to treat all individuals in a non-discriminatory manner, without regard to their protected status under Federal law, regulation or policy. We are committed to the principles of equality, fairness, and respectful treatment for our coworkers and applicants for employment.

This policy applies to all CBP employment programs and management practices and decisions. Additionally, individuals who file complaints alleging unlawful employment discrimination shall not be subject to any form of reprisal.

Furthermore, CBP employees shall not engage in any form of unlawful harassment in the workplace or in the performance of their official duties. Prohibited harassment includes, but is not limited to, unwelcome verbal, non-verbal, or physical behavior directed at an individual because of his or her protected status under the law when such actions unreasonably interfere with the person's ability to perform his or her assigned duties. All CBP executives, managers, and supervisors shall take immediate and appropriate action once they are made aware of an allegation of harassment. Please note that even if an individual's behavior does not rise to the level of unlawful discrimination as defined by Federal law, regulation, executive order or policy, it may still violate CBP's Standards of Conduct."

Deputy Commissioner

CBP Directive Standard of Conduct

Conduct Prejudicial to the Government.

"Employees shall not engage, on or off duty, in criminal, infamous, dishonest, or notoriously disgraceful conduct, or any other conduct prejudicial to the government."

Prohibited Actions.

"Employees will avoid any action, whether or not specifically prohibited by these Standards of Conduct, which might result in, or reasonably create the appearance of:

- Using public service for private gain.
- Giving preferential treatment to a private organization or individual in connection with official government duties and/or responsibilities.
- Impeding government efficiency or economy.
- Engaging in activities which conflict with official government duties and/or responsibilities."

Disclosure and Safeguarding of Official Information.

"Employees must safeguard all sensitive information against unauthorized disclosure, alteration, or loss. Unauthorized accessing of these systems, including "browsing" (querying the systems for information for other than official reasons) is also prohibited."

"Employees will not access, conceal, alter, remove, mutilate, or destroy documents or data in the custody of CBP or the Federal Government without proper authority."

Office Equipment and Computers.

"Generally, CBP employees may use government office equipment for authorized purposes only. However, limited personal use of government office equipment by employees during non-work time is considered to be an "authorized use" of government property if such use involves only minimal additional expense to CBP and does not: adversely affect the performance of official duties; interfere with the mission or operations of CBP; overburden any CBP information resources; or violate any standard of conduct herein."

Customs and Border Protection Directive

Individual Complaints 29 CFR 1614.106(d)

"A complainant may amend a complaint at any time prior to the conclusion of the investigation to include issues or claims like or related to those raised in the complaint. After requesting a hearing, a complainant may file a motion with the administrative judge to amend a complaint to include issues or claims like or related to those raised in the complaint."

Individual Complaints 29 CFR 1614.106(e)

"The agency shall acknowledge receipt of a complaint or an amendment to a complaint in writing and inform the complainant of the date on which the complaint or amendment was filed."

Administrative Grievance System

"It is CBP policy to maintain a climate of openness in which an employee can feel free to express concerns and dissatisfactions and to use the grievance system for their resolution. It is also CBP policy to afford covered employees' ample opportunity to obtain consideration of issues concerning matters personally affecting them which are subject to management control.

Definition

<u>Grievance</u>: A written request by an employee, or a group of employees, for resolution of a matter of concern and/or dissatisfaction relating to the employment and/or conditions of employment of the employee(s), which is subject to the control of CBP management."

CBP Directive

Freedom of Information Act

"What is FOIA? Enacted on July 4, 1966, and taking effect one year later, the Freedom of Information Act (FOIA) provides that any person has a right, enforceable in court, to obtain access to federal agency records, except to the extent that such records (or portions of them) are protected from public disclosure by one of none exemptions or by one of three special law enforcement record exclusion. A FOIA request can be made for any agency record. Before sending a request to a federal agency, you should determine which agency is likely to have the records you are seeking. Each agency's website will contain information about the type of records that agency maintains.

The FOIA is a law that gives you the right to access information from the federal government. It is often described as the law that keeps citizens in the know about their government. Under the FOIA, agencies must disclose any information that is requested – unless that information is protected from public disclosure. The FOIA also requires that agencies automatically disclose certain information, including frequently requested records. As Congress, the President, and the Supreme Court have all recognized, the FOIA is a vital part of our democracy.

Who oversees the FOIA? It is the Executive Branch, led by the President, that is responsible for the administration of the FOIA across the government. The Department of Justice's Office of Information Policy oversees agency compliance with these directives and encourages all agencies to fully comply with both the letter and the spirit of the FOIA.

What is the Administration's FOIA Policy? President and Attorney General have directed agencies to apply a presumption of openness in responding to FOIA requests. The Attorney General specifically called on agencies not to withhold information just because it technically falls within an exemption and he also encouraged agencies to make discretionary releases of records. The Attorney General emphasized that the President has called on agencies to work in a spirit of cooperation with FOIA requesters. The Office of Information Policy at the Department of Justice oversees agency compliance with these directives and encourages all agencies to fully comply with both the letter and the spirit of the FOIA. The President has pledged to make this the most transparent Administration in history."

FOIA.GOV

Freedom of Information Act Requests

1. "The FOIA provides that any person has the right to request access to Federal agency records or information.

2. All agencies of the United States government are required to disclose records upon receiving a written request for them, except for those records that are protected from disclosure by the nine exemptions and three special law enforcement record exclusions.

3. The right of access if enforceable in court.

4. The FOIA Division is responsible for acknowledging and responding to requests within 20 business days (excluding Saturdays, Sundays, and legal holidays) as required by statute.

5. The FOIA Division may extend the response time for an additional ten business days when:
   a. The division needs time to collect responsive records from field offices;
   b. The request involves a "voluminous" amount of records which must be located, compiled, and reviewed; or
   c. The division must consult with another agency, which as a substantial interest in the responsive material or amount two or more offices of CBP.
   d. FOIA requests that are maintained in national computer systems, and are accessible to the FOIA staff, are processed independently by the FOIA Division.
   e. Prior to responding to a FOIA request, the DCR FOIA representative shall ensure that

she or he has received and reviewed a copy of the incoming request and a copy of the acknowledgement letter transmitted to the requestor by the FOIA Division.

f. The DCR FOIA representative will prepare an email memorandum acknowledging receipt of the request and submit it electronically to the CBP FOIA Office within two (2) business days of DCR's receipt of the request. The Executive Director, DCR will be copied on the acknowledgment memorandum.

g. The DCR FOIA representative should always adhere to the deadlines requested by the entity making the request of CR, even if the deadline is earlier than the ten (10) business day's deadline set internally by DCR.

6. In assessing whether or not DCR has any records responsive to the request, the DCR FOIA representative must consider whether or not the records fall within any of the legal exemptions established by the FOIA. The exemptions under the FOIA are:

a. Specifically authorized under criteria established by an Executive Order to be kept secret in the interest of national defense or foreign policy, and classified pursuant to such order;

b. Information relating solely to the internal personnel rules and practices of an agency;

c. Information specifically exempted from disclosure by statute (other than 5 U.S.C.

552(b)), if the statute requires that the matters be withheld from the public in such a manner as to leave no discretion on the issue or established particular criteria for withholding or refers to particular types of matters to be withheld.

d. Trade secrets and commercial or financial information obtained from any person which is privileged or confidential;

e. Interagency or intra-agency memoranda or letters which would not be available by law to a private party in litigation with the agency;

f. Personnel and medical files and similar files the disclosure of which would constitute a clearly unwarranted invasion of personal privacy;

g. Records or information compiled for law enforcement purposes, but only to the extent that the production of such enforcement records or information could reasonably be expected to interfere with enforcement proceedings, or deprive a person of a right to a fair trial or an impartial adjudication, or could reasonably be expected to constitute an unwarranted invasion of personal privacy, or could reasonably be expected to disclose the identity of a confidential source, or including a State, local or foreign agency or authority or any private institute which furnished the information on a confidential basis, or would disclose techniques or procedures, or disclose guidelines for law enforcement investigations or prosecutions, or could reasonably be expected to endanger the life or physical safety of any individual;

h. Information contained in or related to examination, operating, or condition reports prepared by or for any agency responsible for the regulations or supervision of financial institutions;

i. Geological and geophysical information and data, including maps, concerning wells.

7. If the DCR representative determines that DCR cannot make a full disclosure, they must also consider whether DCR can make a partial disclosure. Where partial disclosure is possible, the DCR representative should review and redact the responsive records consistent with DHS and CBP policy and procedures.

8. The DCR FOIA representative will close out the FOIA request by preparing a response to the originator of the request; e.g. the FOIA Division or OES, within ten (10) business days of receiving the request or by the deadline imposed by the FOIA Division or OES if sooner. The response will be signed by the Executive Director, DCR and include either;

a. A certification that DCR has no records responsive to the request;

b. DCR has records responsive to the request, but they are exempt for release under the FOIA, along with a specific exemption number(s) and explanation; or

    c. DCR has records responsive to the request, along with a copy of the records redacted in accordance with DHS and CBP policy and procedure.

9. The memorandum of response should indicate the amount of time the DCR FOIA representative expended on conducting the search for the records.
10. The memorandum of response will also request that a copy of the agency's final response to the requestor be forwarded to DCR.
11. The DCR FOIA Representative will provide a bi-weekly report to the Executive Director, Field Directors and Assistant Directors on the status and number of FOIA requests passed."

Privacy and Diversity Office

Reporting Misconduct

"The Joint Intake Center (JIC) serves as the central "clearinghouse" for receiving, processing and tracking allegations of misconduct involving personnel and contractors employed by Customs and Border Protection (CBP) and Immigration and Customs Enforcement (ICE). The JIC provides CBP and ICE with a centralized and uniform system for processing reports of alleged misconduct. All reports of misconduct are coordinated with the Department of Homeland Security (DHS) Office of Inspector General (OIG) and referred to the appropriate office for investigation, fact-finding or immediate management action.

Bear in mind that reports of alleged misconduct may not result in any immediate action or overt signs of activity. Do not assume a lack of visible activity means your report has been ignored or met with indifference. All reports, including those submitted anonymously, receive prompt and complete attention. Employees are subject to disciplinary action for failing to report allegations of misconduct. Allegations of misconduct are to be immediately reported."

Joint Intake Center

Rules of Behavior

"System access is given only to those systems to which an employee is require access in the performance of official duties.

1. Employees are not to access systems they are not authorized to access.
2. Employees will protect sensitive information from disclosure to unauthorized persons or groups.
3. Department of Homeland Security office equipment is to be used for official proposes with only limited personal use allowed."

Department of Homeland Security

Equal Employment Opportunity Pre-Complaint Processing Resolution

"If informal resolution is not possible, the EEO Counselor must hold a final interview with the aggrieved person and issue the Notice of Right to File a Discrimination Complaint. No further counseling should occur."

Management Directive 110

Directions for Completion Checklist Intake of Informal EEO Complaints

<u>Assignment Log</u> "will be utilized to track"

Office of Diversity and Civil Rights

Roles and Responsibilities of an EEO Counselor

"When an aggrieved person seeks EEO counseling, the Counselor must ensure that the complainant understands his or her rights and responsibilities in the EEO process, including the option to elect Alternative Dispute Resolution (ADR). The EEO Counselor must perform several tasks in all cases, regardless of whether the individual ultimately elects the ADR option, including:

1. Advise the aggrieved person about the EEO complaint process.
2. Determine the claim(s) and basis(es) raised by the potential complaint.

3. Conduct an inquiry during the initial interview with the aggrieved person for the purposes of determining jurisdictional questions.

4. Use of the term "initial interview" in this context is not intended to suggest that during the first meeting with the aggrieved person and EEO Counselor must obtain all of the information she or he needs to determine the claim(s) or basis(es).

5. Seek a resolution.

6. Advise the aggrieved person of his or her right to file a formal discrimination complaint if attempts to resolve the dispute through EEO counseling or ADR fail to resolve the dispute.

7. Prepare a report sufficient to document that the EEO Counselor undertook the required counseling actions and to resolve any jurisdictional questions that arise".

U.S. Equal Employment Opportunity Commission

Notification of Time Limits

1. "There are statutory requirements for processing complaints in a timely manner. You must meet them or risk having your complaint dismissed for failure to meet filing requirements.

2. Refer to the EEO Complaint Process flow chart for specific filing requirements".

U.S Customs and Border Protection

Burden of Proof

1. "The evidence you presented in the prima facie context is not sufficient to win a judgement in your favor. You must present evidence to overcome, CBP's rebuttal of your claims and convincingly demonstrate the existence of discrimination.
2. The ultimate standard you must address to prevail is whether it is more likely than not that a violation of Federal law and DHS policy has occurred. You have the burden of persuasion to convince the judge or jury that the facts are true, i.e., prove your case.
3. The final analysis will be made based on the preponderance of the evidence, which refers to the quality and reliability of the evidence and the credibility of the witnesses".

U.S. Customs and Border Protection

Burden of Production (Prima Facie Case)

1. "Federal law and DHS policy prohibits CBP from treating applicants or employees differently (disparate treatment) because of their membership in a protected class: race, color, religion, sex, national origin, age, disability (physical/mental), reprisal (for previous EEO activity), genetic testing, status as a parent, and sexual orientation.
2. In situations where you believe you have received disparate treatment, you have the burden of producing evidence to establish a

prima facie case of discrimination. This means that you must have enough evidence to raise the inference that your allegations are true.

3. After you have established a prima facie case, CBP has the burden of producing evidence to show a legitimate, non-discriminatory reason for its actions, i.e., its actions were not motivated by discrimination.

4. If CBP can show your claims are unfounded, then the burden of producing evidence shifts back to you".

U.S. Customs and Border Protection

Pretext

1. "If CBP has rebutted your prima facie case, you must then show that CBP's stated reason was a mere mask to cover the discriminatory motive.

2. To prevail, you must prove that CBP treated you differently from similarly situated employees in the same chain of command or in the same work unit or that CBP's explanation for the adverse action is false".

U.S. Customs and Border Protection

Representation

"Throughout the EEO process, you have a right to the representative of your choice. At the hearing stage, CBP counsel will represent management".

U.S. Customs and Border Protection

Definition of Reprisal

"You must establish a prima facie case of reprisal by showing:

1. You previously engaged in a protected activity or opposed unlawful discrimination;
2. CBP was aware of your activity;
3. You were subsequently adversely affected by some action of CBP;
4. Some reasonable connection exists between your activity and the adverse employment decision, or
5. You have direct evidence that shows discriminatory intent".

U.S. Customs and Border Protection

Definition of Harassment

1. "Harassment violates Federal law and DHS policy if it is sufficiently severe/pervasive to alter the conditions of employment and create a hostile work environment. Harassment cases are judged using the reasonable person standard; that is, would a reasonable person find the conduct substantially affected the work environment".
2. "Discriminatory harassment is legally defined as verbal or physical conduct that denigrates or shows hostility or aversion toward an individual, or group of individuals, because of race, color, sex (sexual harassment), national origin, age, religion, disability, reprisal, genetic testing, sexual orientation, or status as a parent,

and creates an intimidating, hostile or offensive work environment or has the purpose or effect of unreasonably interfering with an individual's work performance".

3. "A hostile work environment claim requires showing of a pattern of offensive conduct. The key issues in proving harassment are frequency and severity. When considering the claim of a hostile environment, the court also considers the context in which the behavior was exhibited".

4. "In most instances, a single incident (includes isolated incidents) of offensive behavior may not create a hostile environment. If a coworker asks you for a date only one time, it may not be harassment. Use of a racial/ethnic epithet or slur on one occasion may not sufficiently affect working conditions to establish a claim of harassment".

U.S. Customs and Border Protection

Definition of Misconduct

1. "A legal term meaning a wrongful, improper, or unlawful conduct motivated by premeditated or intentional purpose".

2. "Misconduct in the workplace generally falls under two categories. Minor misconduct is seen as unacceptable but is not a criminal offense (e.g. being late). Gross misconduct can lead to dismissal, (e.g. stealing or sexual harassment)."

Wikipedia Encyclopedia

Moving Forward

B ecause of the emotional abuse I went through on my job, my quality of life changed, especially with my family, and in particular, my brother for whom I cared for over twenty years passed away during my employment. My concentration was on my job to survive, but it got to the point that my medical professional requested that I retire. I am young, I can still continue to work, and I want to work, but this job has taken a toll on me physically and mentally; retirement was my only choice.

I remember one day I was at work and it started to snow, and snow heavy. The government was shutting down. A lot of employees from my office started leaving between 1:00 p.m. and 2:00 p.m., to include where I was located. I was wondering why I did not get approval to leave. I had employees call me up and say we are leaving and for me to leave because it was getting bad. I could not leave until my supervisor, Supervisor 7 tell me because if I did, I would have received disciplinary action from leaving work without approval. I waited and waited and waited until 4:25 p.m., when Supervisor 7 called me to say I could leave. Mind you, my work day ended at 4:30 p.m. I had to walk about 7 blocks, catch the train to my car and drive home. The scariest part was going up a hill. I prayed that I did not slide back to hit other cars. My foot stayed on the brakes so long that my leg started shacking. I got up that hill and made it home. What a night.

I never thought how successful I was because of the "bring Penny down" actions. Life after working for the Department of Homeland Security, Customs and Border Protection, Equal Employment Opportunity Office encompasses going through a healing process, which include writing this book to tell my story to you in hopes for a positive change for others. Now that I have retired, I can move forward and enjoy life, have fun, and love as God planned.

I like to leave you with this, It's My Time. God has planted seeds of greatness on the inside of me. He has predestined that those things in my heart will come to pass. I may have had more than my share of unfair things happen in my life. I probably have plenty of reasons to just settle where I am. But understand, the depth of my past is an indication of the height of my future. In other words, if I have been through a lot of negative things in the past, it just means that my future is bigger and brighter and greater than I can even imagine. It's my time to step out and embrace all that God has for me.

Senior Pastor Lakewood Church

CPSIA information can be obtained
at www.ICGtesting.com
Printed in the USA
FSHW011703281019
63481FS

9 781545 653319